A Pilgrimage
Around Wales

'The subtitle of this book is *In Search of a Significant Conversation*, and its contents cause us to appreciate... the conversations, random or otherwise, which peppered the author's pilgrimage around Wales. Unspoken or spoken, those conversations bring the places to life, and illuminate the faith which motivated the journey.'

The Most Reverend John D E Davies
Bishop of Swansea & Brecon and Archbishop of Wales

'Those of us who have been entertained, informed, and spiritually stirred by Anne's talks on her pilgrimages will be delighted that her reflections on walking in Wales are brought together and made available for a far wider audience to enjoy.'

Revd Canon Dr Sarah Rowland Jones LVO OBE
The City Church of St John the Baptist, Cardiff

'"Camping here is my gift to you," said one campsite owner to Anne on her tremendous pilgrimage, and this book is a real gift to us, with Anne's thoughts reminding us of the vast riches we have in Wales in so many ways.

With her historical and spiritual reflections, we are taken on the pilgrimage with her, having the opportunity to join in with that journey of discovery and prayer.

With Anne we visit many churches of different sizes and traditions but more importantly we meet the people that make up the family of the church and the family of Wales. A really engaging and interesting book.'

Revd Canon Ian Rees
Rector of Central Swansea

A Pilgrimage
Around Wales

IN SEARCH OF A SIGNIFICANT CONVERSATION

A N N E   H A Y W A R D

To Martin, with all my thanks

First impression: 2018

Front cover photographs: Wikimedia Commons
(St David's Cathedral – JKMMX;
Bardsey Island – Keith Ruffles;
St Illtud's Church, Llantwit Major – John Salmon;
St Melangell's Church, Pennant Melangell – Rhys Williams;
St Winifride's Well, Holywell – Alex Liivet)
All other photographs: Anne Hayward
Cover design: Y Lolfa

ISBN: 978 1 78461 529 1

Published and printed in Wales
on paper from well-maintained forests by
Y Lolfa Cyf., Talybont, Ceredigion SY24 5HE
website www.ylolfa.com
e-mail ylolfa@ylolfa.com
tel 01970 832 304
fax 832 782

CONTENTS

My route around Wales

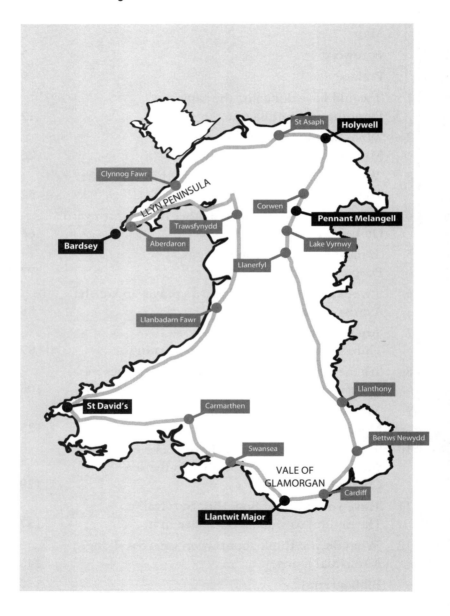

Foreword

PILGRIMAGE MUST PROPERLY be distinguished from tourism. The latter is usually a 'bald' encounter with a place, a person or even an artefact. The former is an encounter with another, or with 'the other', in a Christian sense: an encounter with God, often triggered by an encounter with a place, a person or a thing. One of my abiding hopes is that some who come as tourists to any number of the holy places, grand or simple, with which the land of Wales is blessed, may find themselves there engaged in conversations which begin to take them beyond being tourists and into the territory of becoming pilgrims.

Such conversations are at best personal, but may be silent, the other party being long gone as a physical presence from the place, though still very present in both spirit and texture. In the uncovering of the history of the place and its former people, the voice of the past, frequently the voice of faith, is heard speaking in and through the silence. My most profound personal experience of this phenomenon occurred during a recent pilgrimage to Rome which included a highly privileged visit to the *scavi*, the site of excavations in the Necropolis beneath the Basilica of St Peter, in Rome. With a few others, I was permitted to view not the splendour so readily associated with the Basilica, but, way beneath the great altar which sits at the heart of the Basilica, in a tiny niche in a crude hole in the rock, a number of small containers in which were held a few fragments of bone: verifiably, and beyond any reasonable doubt, physical remains of the body of the Apostle Peter. The presence of the Apostle, the witness of the Apostle, the courage of the Apostle, the love of the Apostle for the Lord and much, much more, were all around in an unspoken conversation triggered by the place, what it held and who it held. Each one of us there sensed continuity of belief and affirmation of faith rooted in the experience of one of Christ's fishermen.

On the same pilgrimage, we visited a number of other holy sites, including places of residence, places of martyrdom, places of worship. In many of them, helpful guides told us stories of the places while, in silence, the people who are no longer there spoke to us and affirmed us in the validity and meaning of our greater pilgrimage as part of the People of God today.

The subtitle of this book is *In Search of a Significant Conversation*, and its contents cause us to appreciate such unspoken conversations as those to which I've just referred, as well as to appreciate the conversations, random or otherwise, which peppered the author's pilgrimage around Wales. Unspoken or spoken, those conversations bring the places to life, and illuminate the faith which motivated the journey.

Those who are personally familiar with the places visited will, particularly, be able to picture many of the scenes described, perhaps imagine the conversations themselves, and even identify with the kind of characters encountered – most of them welcoming and hospitable, some questioning, curious and provocative.

Familiar or not, may both place and conversation come to life together with the faith and the Lord for which and for whom the place came to be. May they enrich, challenge and stimulate you to live out that faith in both its challenges and its grace.

The Most Reverend John D E Davies
Bishop of Swansea & Brecon and Archbishop of Wales
March 2018

Preface

I WAS VERY fortunate – 'blessed' is a more apt word, perhaps –
to have been able to take time out of ordinary life in the spring
and summer of 2015 to go on a pilgrimage around Wales. This
book is a fruit of that pilgrimage. When I started out, I certainly
didn't intend to write a book about my walk but various factors
along the way persuaded me to attempt to do so.

There are three strands to my writing in this book. The bulk
of the text is composed of responses to the many questions and
comments made to me by different people along the way. The
next category is factual snippets which provide background
information, mostly historical, which I think is relevant or
significant. The third type of writing is reflections on various
spiritual issues that cropped up on my walk. Every chapter
contains all three types of writing, in varying proportions.

In writing this book, there have also been various things
I needed to take into account when considering what others
might make of my efforts.

Firstly, I was very aware as I walked that I was in a culture
different from my own, and the most obvious aspect of this
was the widespread use of Welsh as a living language. There
were times on my pilgrimage when I felt painfully English.

However, in my text, I decided – as a non-Welsh speaker (or
perhaps a very slow Welsh learner) – that I would give place
names as they are used by English speakers. In many cases
the names of towns, villages and other features are the same
for everyone, but in cases where the Welsh name is different to
that used in English, I have put this after the English name but
on my first mention of the place only.

I have also assumed some basic knowledge of areas and

counties of Wales, as it proved impractical to include everything on my map on page 6. I have tried to make sure that all places I mention are placed in the context of cities, towns and villages I have included on the map.

I am also aware that not everyone is familiar with terms used to describe particular periods in history. I especially wanted to make clear that by 'early medieval period' is meant the time between the withdrawal of the Romans in the late fourth century and the coming of the Normans soon after William the Conqueror seized the English throne in 1066. The 'Age of the Saints' is the name given by some to the first two or three hundred years of the early medieval period in Wales. The 'Middle Ages' is the term used from the arrival of the Normans to the end of the fifteenth century, or the coming to power of the Tudor dynasty. Of course, any historical terms for periods of time are, ultimately, only convenient labels.

I also found that when I was talking with people or when I was writing or (heaven forbid!) when I was going over things in my own mind, I used the words 'pilgrimage', 'walk' and 'trek' fairly interchangeably and sometimes combined together. I am, of course, talking about the same journey on foot.

Being on foot, and carrying quite a heavy pack for a small(ish) woman, was both liberating and constraining. The more I walked, and now the more I research and write, it becomes increasingly obvious how little I saw and how many places, in some ideal world, I could have visited. I'm aware that my route didn't include many places that other people may consider significant or important. In addition, of the churches I visited, the majority were Church in Wales (Anglican) churches, which I appreciate is far from representative. However, for all sorts of reasons, this is how things worked out.

What became increasingly clear during those three months was that my research prior to my walk had left me unprepared for the sheer joy of quietly discovering new places and the enormous sense of achievement that I felt each day. Often what was most overwhelming was the beauty of the ordinariness of many of my days.

I'm also aware that whenever I visited a church, or any other place for that matter, I only ever saw a quick snapshot of how things were during those few minutes I was there. A journey such as mine could be seen as rather arrogant; someone with the time and energy to go around 'inspecting' churches. But that wasn't my intention, or the reality. What I saw was a picture of commitment, faithfulness and love for the local expression of the body of Christ.

I seemed to do a lot of planning and preparation before I set out; eventually I realised that I just had to go! My preparations were also dwarfed by the privilege of receiving the interest, kindness and brief companionship of the people I met along the way. It is to these people, and to my patient husband, Martin, that I owe my thanks.

Anne Hayward
March 2018

CHAPTER 1

'I would have done just the same'
PLANNING AND SETTING OUT

'I WOULD HAVE done just the same if I'd been younger and fitter and had the opportunity,' remarked an elderly lady from the passenger seat of the car driven by her rather younger husband. I met this couple on the first day of my walk; we had got talking after they asked me for directions to the remote Black Mountains church it turned out we were all heading for. This conversation and my declining of the lift they offered me gave me a brief opportunity, the first of very many, to say that I had embarked on a pilgrimage around Wales on foot.

The surprising heat of the April day, the steepness of the road and the considerable distance I had still to cover beyond the church made me later regret not asking them to carry my backpack to our mutual destination. However, the lady's warm words of affirmation were a great encouragement at this point. About two and a half hours into the first day of my pilgrimage around Wales and clearly only a few miles from home, I had three months ahead of me to complete my objective; a timescale dictated by the very practical reason that I needed to be home to look after family members visiting from New Zealand.

I had begun to plan and think through my pilgrimage exactly a year before I set out, although the idea of doing a long prayer walk across Wales had been in my mind for a few years before that. In my notebook I had listed my reasons for doing a pilgrimage. Revisiting that list, I found it as follows:

- For some time I have felt called to a life with a greater commitment to prayer
- I'm interested in the early years of Christianity in Britain and what they can teach us
- I'm interested in the lives of the early saints and the way they expressed their faith
- I've tried to learn about Welsh history and would like to build on that
- I've lived on the English border with Wales for a considerable part of my life and I think of myself as from the 'Marches'[1]
- I'm interested in pilgrimage both in history and in the contemporary world
- I'm already a (reasonable) long-distance walker
- I want to find a more peaceful, more reflective and happier place in my life

Such were the reasons I had noted down a year before I actually set out. Of course, there were unwritten reasons too: I had decided to give up my teaching job and move to the Black Mountains area of Wales, near to my home county of Herefordshire. I was also a little bit envious of the time and opportunities a close family member, one of my sisters to be precise, had to research and write – although I don't suppose she would have seen it that way. I was also beginning to think more about my own vocation as a Christian and what this might involve. Perhaps too there was the feeling that it was the right time to do something different: to have a little bit of an adventure. I was certainly fortunate that various factors combined to give me the freedom not only to relinquish my 'ordinary' job but also allowed me to take on a project of this type. The health and strength I needed was clearly an essential factor which I was blessed to enjoy. Simple practical things also worked for me: one of my sons was a keen walker who had trekked across Scotland and Norway, and on two short trips had taken me with him. This gave me the confidence to walk and camp on my own and also meant I had the right equipment; a lightweight tent, a tiny stove and – my pride and joy – an extremely compact and also very comfortable inflatable airbed. I was also a reasonable navigator and confident enough with maps to get myself around remote areas.

However, there was another reason lurking somewhere in my planning. At the start this had not really featured in my thinking, but as I approached the time I'd set for my departure, the potential for getting into conversations with people along the way began to grow as an idea in my mind. A year or two before, I had felt God was leading me to pray for a significant conversation each day. I had become aware that much of my talk with others was mundane or businesslike. Praying for a significant conversation each day opened up for me a fresh way to relate to others, particularly with my wider family and work colleagues. Sometimes I knew as we were speaking that I was engaged in that day's significant conversation, but on other occasions it wasn't obvious until later, as I reflected on the day's events. Occasionally there was more than one such conversation in a day – and perhaps there were others whose significance I didn't recognise, but which were meaningful to the other person.

In all the activity of moving house and to a new area, I'd forgotten to pray and look for those conversations which in small ways had given me all sorts of opportunities to hear about the lives and concerns of others and for me, in small ways, to share my faith. But as the day of my departure drew near, I had a growing sense that my pilgrimage would give me opportunities for significant conversations. In fact, the conversations far exceeded my expectations and, for me, almost became the purpose of my walking, hence the subtitle of this book.

And so, not without apprehension, I approached the date I had set for leaving: the Tuesday after Easter. Leaving at Easter had been my objective from when I had begun more detailed planning, but, family guests having left, very warm days also encouraged me at the start. Chaucer speaks of April as a month when 'longen folk to gon on pilgrimages'[2], and it seemed a good idea to me too.

> **Come and see**
>
> Look at the story, in the first chapter of John's gospel, of the sceptical Nathanael meeting Jesus, having earlier complained 'Can any good thing come out of Nazareth?' We too may feel we're surrounded by the sceptical, the cynical or just the indifferent. But Nathanael's friend Philip had already met Jesus, 'Him of whom Moses in the Law and also the Prophets wrote'. He urged Nathanael to 'Come and see'. We too can reach out to people in a straightforward, natural way and suggest they 'Come and see'. It may not seem that we have something to share with others, but we do. And that something is a person, the Jesus we can all encourage others to 'Come and see'. My walk gave me many natural opportunities to make that simple invitation.

'How do you know where to go?'

Quite early in the planning of my pilgrimage, I decided to make the four main ancient places of pilgrimage in Wales the key points of my walk: that is, Holywell (*Treffynnon*), the island of Bardsey (*Ynys Enlli*), St David's (*Tyddewi*) and Llantwit Major (*Llanilltud Fawr*). I was aware that this implied some value judgements on my part, as there are other places that could be seen as equally significant. These four places were conveniently more or less in the 'corners' of Wales and so my pilgrimage could become a roughly circular walk, taking in many different areas and types of terrain. After that I searched online and in various books for information about sites that were believed to go back to the Age of the Saints[3].

At the start these were mainly church sites and holy wells, although later I researched more about ancient yew trees and inscribed stones. I also allowed myself to do some research about Roman sites and a few Iron Age and Bronze Age ones. Inevitably, I also found some later medieval sites and indeed places of interest from more modern times. However, I tried to focus on the Age of the Saints as otherwise I would have been overwhelmed by possibilities. As well as building up computer files, I got an old road atlas and some mini post-it notes. I wrote very brief notes on the post-its as regards potential places to visit and stuck them on the relevant place on the road atlas, the scale of which proved ideal for this purpose. A rough itinerary soon began to emerge.

I then searched for possible places to camp online, in a few camping books and where indicated on Ordnance Survey maps. I aimed to have a steady trickle of places to stay and noted these down in my notebook, allowing a page or two for each OS map. When I felt I had enough information on places to visit, I then transferred the post-it notes into the relevant page in my notebook. I had also intended, when I first started researching my route, to use old roads, pilgrim routes and green lanes. In practice this was difficult, partly because it would have required a degree of expertise and research skills that I didn't really have, although it certainly seemed like a nice idea at the start.

I also faced the constraints of my own strength and fitness. I decided to aim to walk ten to twelve miles a day, which seemed realistic given that I needed to keep this up for three months for often six days a week. However, the need to get to a campsite each night was the determining factor a lot of the time, resulting sometimes in long days of perhaps fifteen miles and other days which were only half that length. The hilliness of the terrain I was going through was also an issue. I found that climbing one major or two lesser hills per day was more than enough.

Wales is fortunate in having a well-established walking route around the country's long coastline but, in practice, I found walking on the Wales Coastal Path particularly tiring and rarely did this for more than a few miles at a time. People also often ask me if I walked up the Offa's Dyke (*Clawdd Offa*) Path, which roughly follows the eastern border with England. However, the route I took was some distance to the west of

Offa's Dyke and I only used this long distance trail for a few miles in north-east Wales.

I roughly aimed to visit one significant place each day, and this was nearly always the case. There were just a few days when I focussed on covering ground, and even these often led to lovely and interesting surprises. It was probably the case that my walk was defined almost as much by what I couldn't get to see as what I did visit, and perhaps this was inevitable. I had also originally intended to visit the large and very interesting island of Anglesey and spend perhaps three days there. However, quite unexpectedly, I ended up walking across north Wales with a group of pilgrims who did that route every year. If I wanted to stay with them, I obviously had to follow their itinerary, which did not include Anglesey. Walking with the pilgrim group seemed an opportunity that was too good to pass up on, and so the island was missed out. It did not seem practical to then go back to Anglesey, which is worth a serious pilgrimage in its own right.

Walking with this pilgrim group also clarified my own route across north Wales, as they were following a route they

A choir of teddy bears in the Black Mountains.

had devised over the previous few years[4]. I was aware of the existence of this route from my research, but if I had been walking on my own I would probably have had to deviate from it due to the lack of places to camp. I would have needed to stay closer to the coast to make use of the facilities there. However, walking with others meant that for at least some of the time, I could fit in with the accommodation they had planned for themselves.

As regards the 'micro-planning' of my route, tiny lanes indicated in yellow with a broken edge on Ordnance Survey maps[5] proved invaluable, as on these you have an absolute and inarguable right to be there, it's easy to navigate and the surface is always going to be OK. In much of Wales there is hardly any traffic on these roads and it often feels like your own private walking track. There was usually also a steady trickle of people about, although there were exceptions to this in some remote areas. However, I did notice as I approached the more urban south east of Wales and the Cardiff (*Caerdydd*) and Newport (*Casnewydd*) area that this classification of road became busier and less common.

I was also able to use some stretches of National Trails[6]. These are generally well signposted, clearly shown on OS maps and are in reasonably regular use. I used a little of the Wye Valley Walk near Builth Wells (*Llanfair ym Muallt*), the Glendower Way around the area of Lake Vyrnwy (*Llyn Efyrnwy*) and the Offa's Dyke Path over the Clwydian Hills on the first section of my walk to Holywell. In the second half of my pilgrimage, as I made my way down to St David's, I used some of the Wales Coast Path. I also benefitted in some more remote areas from the open access allowed on uplands and mountains in much of Wales, notably when I set out and as I approached home in the hills of Monmouthshire and the Black Mountains, and on the rather bleak expanses above Pennant Melangell in the north of the county of Powys.

I was also able on some occasions to use byways and green lanes[7]; indeed, when I started out, I intended mainly using such routes. But although these often very old roads were usually clearly signposted in my own area, as I moved north into mid Wales this proved not to be the case. I was anxious not to trespass and the situation was complicated by lambing being well underway. After a few tricky days I decided to focus on using lanes and clearly marked national trails rather than risk time and energy lost in terrain that was often difficult and tiring to navigate. I often had to remind myself that I was doing a pilgrimage rather than an ordinary mountain or cross country walk. The places that I wanted to visit were also nearly always on roads and in villages and towns rather than on high level or mountainous routes.

I was also affected by my own personal preferences and sometimes by unforeseen circumstances. On the Llŷn Peninsula in north Wales I was close to places where I had, on many occasions, been on holiday as a child and which held tremendous memories for me. However, these memories seemed to complicate my pilgrimage and intrude on it somehow, so in that area I concentrated on places I didn't know well. As a result, I saw lovely and fascinating sites that I knew nothing of; I would probably have missed out on these if I'd focussed on the places that I had known from childhood.

'I am simply speechless'

This was spoken to me after church one Sunday in mid Wales, a couple of months into my walk. The woman making this comment was perhaps in her late thirties and she was the mother of three children who had also all been present at the service. She had asked me about my trip and I had outlined what I had done, leading to this remark. Of course she was not the only person to be surprised by what I was doing, but then I would have been surprised too only a year or so before. Even now, I feel a little amazed that I actually achieved my objective. I think what helped me was dividing my trip up into sections, in my mind at least.

Visiting churches along the way, there was often a visitors' book to sign. For the first couple of weeks, as I approached Pennant Melangell on the first 'leg' of my walk, I wrote in each visitors' book that I was 'On pilgrimage to Pennant Melangell'. Once there, I allowed myself to write that I was 'On pilgrimage to Holywell'. To have written that I was on pilgrimage around Wales in those early days would have seemed presumptuous. When asked about my destination in those first few weeks, I also just talked in terms of the next key point on my pilgrimage, although some more persistent questioners would then ask what my plans were when I'd got to the next major place.

Generally speaking, I made the progress I expected to make and this helped to keep my morale up. Rather unexpectedly walking across north Wales with the pilgrim group I met up with by chance meant that I had to maintain their relatively brisk pace. I covered the distance from Holywell in the east to Aberdaron and Bardsey Island at the tip of the Llŷn Peninsula in two weeks, when I had originally planned to take three.

Good weather certainly helped to keep me positive and my health was generally excellent. I had been concerned that my right knee – which had been quite problematic a few years before – would be affected by so much walking, but it was absolutely fine. I was used to wearing a knee support for any walk over about seven or eight miles, but my knee was so much better than I thought it would be that I hardly wore the support at all.

Another health-related problem was my poor sleeping, which had been an issue all my adult life. I had got used to using over-the-counter sleeping remedies based on anti-histamines for any trip away, as I slept particularly poorly whenever I was away from my own bed. Even at home I often slept badly. Although I had generally been getting better over the year or two before the pilgrimage, I still remember the moment in my planning when I realised that I would need to do the trip without any medication, as these pills are only intended for very short-term use. At the time this seemed like quite a daunting challenge, but it was one I knew I needed to trust God for.

I was delighted that I experienced such healing in this area, sleeping well most of the time, especially when it was cold with long nights on the first leg of my trip. When I did wake up in the night, I found I generally quickly got back to sleep and even when I was awake for a while, I was often so tired that just lying in my sleeping bag was still restful. For someone who has been close to ill with poor sleeping, I would go so far as to say that the improvement I experienced was miraculous.

Although things did deteriorate a little later in the trip, this seemed mainly to be because the nights were very short so I was tending to wake very early, and I also got too hot in the night in my warm sleeping bag. I realised this was one area where I needed to equip myself better: for future trips I needed a lightweight compact sleeping bag for warmer British summer weather. Another factor was the mild hay fever which was one of the factors in my insomnia; however, I only needed to take medication for this on a handful of occasions.

Llanthony

My first day of walking ended at Llanthony Priory near Abergavenny, a few hours' walk further on from the church the couple in the car had been looking for. What is perhaps intriguing about this place is that the dramatic ruins in a beautiful mountain landscape are what survives of a religious house[8] that was itself inspired by much earlier ruins. Out hunting in the lovely Vale of Ewyas in the late eleventh or perhaps early twelfth century, William de Lacy, a retainer and relative of the Norman[9] de Lacy family, came across the remains of what he was told had been the hermitage of St David. Overcome by the peaceful serenity of the place, William dedicated his life to God by living here as a hermit with his companion Ernisius. A decade or so later, they were persuaded to allow their hermitage to expand to become a house of Augustinian canons[10]. Under the Augustinian rule, these men were not monks but all priests who acted as the clergy of churches and chapels in the area. This arrangement lasted for only a generation before local hostility caused the priory to be abandoned, and the canons to seek refuge initially in Hereford and then in the new foundation of Llanthony Secunda in Gloucester. Only in the thirteenth century was the Priory rebuilt and reoccupied; the ruins that are seen today date from this time.

The story of William de Lacy and his hunting trip is known through three medieval writers, two of whom were clerics at the Priory and the third being Gerald of Wales, who visited the site in 1188. It is certainly a story that raises all sorts of questions. One might ask, just what were the ruins that had survived perhaps for five hundred years since the time of St David? Were these ruins of an early Welsh *llan*, with its simple church and huts for a small community? Was this simple settlement itself a development of David's smaller hermitage? In what circumstances had the site been abandoned, and had it perhaps never developed beyond being a hermitage? And although the present thirteenth-century church is traditionally said to be on the site of the ruins seen by William, could the site have been elsewhere in the valley?

Above all, there is the question of how much connection St David actually had with this site. He lived over 500 years before William and nothing connects him to this glorious place apart from the name and the much later medieval account of William and the ruins. The name, Llanthony, is an anglicised corruption of *Llanddewi Nant Honddu* (meaning 'David's church by the Honddu stream'), and the three medieval writers from whom we learn the story seem to have been quite happy to accept the local tradition of St David's presence in the valley. The site may have been used more by his disciples, or perhaps he just spent a short time here.

However, perhaps another remarkable thing about this story is that William de Lacy venerated the memory of St David at all, or at least was portrayed as doing so. St David, like other early Welsh saints, had no formal canonisation at this time. He was not made a saint by the Roman Catholic Church until 1220. This account of a Norman knight being spiritually challenged by the memory of St David as found in the ruins is, as far as I know, a unique and still-powerful story.

Old roads and lanes

Walking in a landscape over reasonable distances and looking for safe and interesting routes is perhaps the best way to begin to observe the old roads and lanes that can easily be overlooked when you're in a car.

One example would be from the morning of the second day of my walk when I walked up the lovely Vale of Ewyas from Llanthony Priory to Capel-y-ffin. Here, over the space of no more than four miles, the track goes through six different sections. which include four different classifications on the Ordnance Survey map, and yet it is all clearly the same route. It's also notable that there are several older houses and farms on this track or very close to it. In contrast, the 'main' road running through the valley, running almost parallel to the track, has very few houses or farms on it. It's also notable that the track is below where the ground becomes steep and stony but above the undulating and possibly damp ground of the land nearer the river. I would go so far as to speculate that this is the original course of the main route through the valley.

Getting to Capel-y-ffin, I then took the left fork, which carries on as a lane for a quite steep mile and a half and then becomes a mountain track going over the ridge of the Black Mountains, down the escarpment on the northern side and then on towards Glasbury (Y Clas-ar-Wy). It becomes a tarmac road again when the ground becomes reasonably level. It's interesting to contrast this with the right fork at Capel-y-ffin, which continues as a tarmac road, again over the ridge of the Black Mountains and then down towards Hay-on-Wye (Y Gelli). Why did one route evolve into a tarmac road while the other never became more than a track?

I would suggest this is because Hay has become a substantial centre in modern times, whereas Glasbury's heyday was in the early medieval period. Physical geography has probably had a role too. The Glasbury route's highest point is about 650 m, whereas the Hay route over the famous Gospel Pass is at 549 m; the 100 m difference in altitude could have made all the difference in winter. Also, the route over towards Hay is more gentle in gradient both before and below the Gospel Pass, making it much more practical for horse-drawn vehicles. I would suggest that the Glasbury route may be older and is, in effect, a lost road that never became part of the modern road system.

Peregrinatio

In the early medieval period, pilgrimage usually meant *perigrinatio*; that is, a spiritual exile, sometimes permanent and sometimes done as a penance. The aim wasn't to get to a particular holy place, but was more a form of spiritual wandering. What we usually think of a pilgrimage – that is, a journey to a specific place of religious significance – does not seem to have become commonplace until the eleventh century or so.

I also found that on several occasions I came across small but unexpected things relevant to pilgrimage. One was at Llanina, a tiny church near New Quay (*Cei Newydd*) on the coast of Ceredigion. It was explained there that the devout King Ine of Wessex was reputedly the founder of the church, having been shipwrecked nearby. Although the story about his connection with this church is disputed, I did find it rather moving that Ine abdicated his throne in order to go on pilgrimage to Rome with his wife in 726.

A few weeks later, when in Llawhaden (*Llanhuadain*) in Carmarthenshire, I also saw the still quite considerable remains of the pilgrim *hospitium*[11], which would have given lodgings and assistance not only to pilgrims and other travellers but also to the sick and destitute. What you can see there today was probably the chapel of what would have been quite a substantial property. This *hospitium* was on the route to St David's and was owned by the monastery there as part of their provision for pilgrims and others as they travelled to the saint's shrine. In addition to the demands of Christian charity, pilgrims brought in considerable income and so providing support for them along the way made financial sense.

In nearby Spittal there was another similar institution; although the building has long since disappeared, the *hospitium* lives on in the place name. Pilgrims going to St David's are also thought to have been responsible for making the pilgrim cross incised into a small cliff face alongside a path near Nevern (*Nanhyfer*) in north Pembrokeshire. Traditionally, pilgrims kiss the cross; in fact the stone is worn away where you need to step up in order to reach it, suggesting that many thousands of pilgrims have passed that way. The cross is now on just a footpath, but it may have been a road hundreds of years ago.

On the hillside above the post-war new town of Cwmbran (*Cwmbrân*) close to the end of my walk, I also saw the rather scant remains of a chapel which belonged to the Cistercian abbey at nearby Llantarnam (*Llanfihangel Llantarnam*). This was an old and interesting settlement, but is now in effect a suburb of the larger town.

I came across the site of the old chapel quite unexpectedly, although an information board nearby told me these ruins are part of a 'pilgrim trail' encouraged by the local council[12]. The chapel, believed to be a sixth-century site, was dedicated to St Derfel. It was on the pilgrim route not only to the shrine at Penrhys in Glamorgan, also owned by the abbey, but also to St David's. Nearby Llanderfel Farm preserves the name of the chapel.

The places we didn't go to

At one point I was walking on the Llŷn Peninsula, where I had spent many family holidays as a child. We once counted that we had all been there over twenty times.

Some of the places in this area have very vivid memories for me, and often very happy ones too. Yet when I was in that area, I decided not to visit the beautiful beach and nearby campsite which I had known so well. I felt my memories of that place were so special that I wanted them to stay in the past; as a result, I deliberately went to a few other places in that area that we hadn't been to, or hadn't visited very often.

So I went to the beach my parents considered too windy and unpicturesque, the hills scarred by quarrying (I can still hear my childhood self asking to be taken to these hills and being told it wasn't worth it because of the quarries), the small Victorian seaside resort with its brightly coloured ranks of beach huts, the area taken over by a 'village' of residential caravans, the rather scruffy town with its holiday camp, the place where there was always a traffic jam and so on. Needless to say all these places were interesting to me and I felt something of a sense of adventure as I went to areas that had been off limits in my childhood.

However, I can see that my parents had some good reasons for not wanting to go to these seemingly less attractive spots: the windy beach would have been a dangerous place for us as children to swim, for example. But as I walked through that area, it was good to exert some independence and be a 'new creation'.

CHAPTER 2

'What do you have in your pack?'
MY PACK AND THE PRACTICALITIES

THIS QUESTION WAS posed to me in a brief conversation in mid Wales. I was walking through the area surrounding the magnificent dam at Lake Vyrnwy – in fact a reservoir constructed in the late Victorian era to supply water for the city of Birmingham. When it was first built, the dam was the largest of its type in Europe. Today it's a Grade I listed structure and, with the large and picturesque reservoir, quite a draw for visitors and tourists.

Heading back through the car park after spending a few minutes in one of the bird hides near the dam, a couple asked me what I had in my pack. Although I had carefully planned what I would take, I had never until that moment been asked what I had with me. I took a brisk and businesslike approach to this question, trying not to get bogged down in the minutiae of what I had.

Using the pack itself as a visual aid, I told them that in the lower section I had my small stove and gas cylinder, a pan and a small supply of food. In the main section of my bag I had my sleeping bag and a few (and it was a very few) spare clothes. These were contained in a 'dry bag' that would prevent them from getting wet in case of bad weather (the pack itself had a rain cover but this only gave protection from showers and not prolonged or heavy rain). A small second dry bag contained a few first aid and emergency items. My inflatable sleep mat also went in the main section of the bag. There were also two smaller pockets, one on each side of the pack. One contained my money and phone in a waterproof wallet. The pocket on the other side contained a few items for washing. In the top of the pack near my head, there was another reasonable-sized pocket which I put my waterproof jacket and trousers in. My water bottle and a lightweight, folding and very useful 'seat' slipped into the mesh pockets on the sides of the pack. I also had a walking stick with me (although I later managed to lose this), which I could attach to my pack. My small tent fitted on the bottom of my pack with straps.

The only thing I carried apart from my pack (and my stick when I needed it) was a waterproof map case which, I have to admit, took on the role of a handbag. Putting things in this was the only way I had to keep them neat, so if I bought a newspaper or acquired tourist literature or similar things, I had to put these in the map case. At times this meant it got quite heavy. There were also maps to go in it, of course – sometimes three or even more. On one occasion I posted three maps back to my husband in order to reduce the weight of maps I and the map case were carrying. All my kit survived the trip very well, except this item, which gave way under the strain (I was sometimes putting more fragile food like bread rolls in it too!), and the bag for my tent, which also began to fall apart. For this I had to substitute a bag meant to hold a sleeping bag, which worked very well as a replacement. I also had to acquire a new map holder.

A few people along the way also remarked how small my pack was for someone who was carrying all they needed for a week or so at a time, barring a few food purchases. In contrast, early on my walk I met a man walking the length of the River Wye. As I approached, I could see he was carrying a pack far bulkier and heavier than mine. We stopped to compare kit, companions on the road for just a few minutes as we were walking in opposite directions.

My brilliant pack had a capacity of 36 litres. I estimated it all weighed about 10–11 kilos, including my tent strapped on the bottom. This was quite a weight for me, as I'm not exactly Mrs Universe. However, packing a bag like this does make you think about what you really need. This clearly has parallels with life as a whole. How much do we acquire, and why? Would we feel less burdened if we accumulated fewer material things? What is genuinely important?

I must admit that I did take a certain pleasure in being able to carry everything I needed. I had considered buying a bigger pack for my pilgrimage, but decided against this as the pack itself would have weighed more and there would have been a temptation to take things I didn't really need. However, I had only used my pack for short trips before I went on my pilgrimage and I knew I needed to make more space for a few extra clothes and a few emergency items. I did this by buying a lighter, more compact and rather pricy sleeping bag[13] and by getting a very lightweight waterproof jacket. These were the only two items, apart from some of my maps, that I bought specially for the walk.

Most of the time I was walking on my own. However, I wasn't quite as solitary as I may have appeared, as every week or so my husband arrived in our camper van with supplies of a few food staples, clean socks and so on. He would feed me lots of lovely meals, we would take a day off together and then he would go on his way back home. This was clearly a great support. Only on a few occasions, for example, did I need to wash clothes or buy the small gas canisters I needed for my stove, as I had some of these things in the van.

I also had a selection of lighter clothes to replace the warm things I needed in the first half of my pilgrimage. I had started out in a very warm April, but with freezing temperatures at night. I was very glad of winter clothes, notably a very warm down jacket. May was surprisingly chilly and rather wet but June was very hot, enabling me to carry and wear fewer and lighter clothes.

My burden

When I arrived at Pennant Melangell a couple of weeks into my walk, I had the first opportunity on my pilgrimage to spend a day without my backpack. This was such a novelty that I wrote about my pack and what it meant to me. So on that day in the quiet but curiously warm and almost cluttered church I wrote as follows:

> I am here without a burden today. Today I am free of my burden. My burden is now my life. On the flat it's not too bad, but uphill I walk at a very slow pace; in fact pace is quite the wrong word. My burden is contained in my lovely rucksack. About 10 kilos ('Lighter than I thought,' says the strong farmer who picks it up for me). I have everything I need, but it's still a burden. But it is a burden that guides, directs and leads me with my maps; that feeds me with its stove, fuel and food; that I can lean on in steep places with my stick; that keeps me from the rain with my (as yet unused!) waterproofs; that shelters me with my precious little tent; that watches over me with my first aid and emergency kit; that provides for me to purchase when I come across a shop; that keeps me warm and clean with a few spare clothes, soap, comb and toothbrush; that, when I occasionally stumble into phone reception, enables me to text my loved one with reassurance; that even allows me to recharge my phone for those rare moments. A burden too that provides me with God's word: a little New Testament, and the Old Testament on my phone. It's a burden that gives me notebooks and pen to write down my memories and thoughts.

A few weeks later, in a church on the north Wales coast, I saw a poster for a charity called Shelterbox. Their aim was to raise money to send emergency kits to be used by refugee families in Nepal, which had at that time recently suffered a major earthquake. Each kit included a simple but large tent, cooking utensils, a stove, water-purifying equipment and activities for children. It struck me that these kits were not unlike the contents of my backpack, except that I was making my journey and living in a tent out of choice.

'What do you read in the evenings?'

This was the question posed to me by Jackie, who owned the small paddock next to the rather quirky campsite where I had pitched my tent. She was doing some DIY on a small chalet in her paddock and she beckoned me over, hoping to borrow a Swiss army knife from me to open a tin of paint with. When I explained that I didn't have a Swiss Army knife or anything similar and that my only knife was a green plastic 'spork', she remarked, 'What sort of camper are you?' But Jackie didn't dwell on how she would open the tin of paint; instead she asked me what I read in the evenings. I have to admit that I didn't just tell Jackie the truth: that my main reading matter was my little New Testament. This was a small red Bible issued by the Gideons[14] to school children. As a secondary teacher of Religious Education in what was by then just a distant past life, I had several of these handy little books.

I simply didn't have the courage at that time to say that my main reading matter was the Bible. Although in one sense the reply I gave her was not that untrue in that I mainly read the Bible in the mornings. In the evenings, by the time I had put up my tent, had a cup of tea, made a meal, written my diary and planned my walking for the next day, there was little time or energy left to read.

When I admitted (this bit was true) that, if anything, I read tourist leaflets I had picked up during the day, Jackie looked at me with pity and said she would lend me her library books. I hardly had time to protest that this just wasn't necessary when she popped back to her home nearby, reappearing with three quite large books. Trying to keep my pack as lightweight as possible, this was a situation I hadn't anticipated. Jackie explained to me that all the books contained plays, one being a collection of modern Welsh drama. I have to admit that although carrying these books seemed quite impractical, the thought of doing some more satisfying reading did appeal.

I explained to Jackie that I would take just one of the books which, as she had told me, I would be able to return to any library in the county. So I started to read *The Radicalisation of Bradley Manning* by Tim Price, which I found very interesting.[15] I didn't manage to read any of the other plays in the same volume. I returned the book a few days later to the local library in St David's.

My usual morning reading was from the New Testament. I quite often did not leave my campsite until 10 a.m. or so, mainly because I enjoyed my Bible reading so much. I've always enjoyed reading the Scriptures, but in my ordinary life this is usually just a passage read by my husband in the mornings as part of our 'quiet time'. We then pray together in what is a routine familiar to many evangelicals. We usually follow a Bible reading scheme with notes. It's often only when I'm on holiday that I do more serious and lengthy reading.

On my pilgrimage I got into the routine of reading after having made myself an early-morning cup of tea. Over the course of the trip I read all the gospels and several of the epistles. Having afterwards made my breakfast, sometimes I would read some more over a second cup of tea. Space meant that I was restricted to the New Testament in book form, but I did have the whole of the Bible in an app on my phone. Sometimes when my phone had plenty of battery charge, I would treat myself to reading a little of the Old Testament in this way: I read the book of Job and some of the Psalms. Using my phone had the advantage of not needing good light. Especially early on in my pilgrimage, the nights were still quite long; my eyesight not being the best and my head torch not especially powerful, reading from a book was restricted to the morning and the very early evening.

You prepare a table before me

Having the use of a table at campsites was something that I really appreciated. As I clearly didn't carry a table and chair with me (I just had a simple, folding mat to sit on), spotting a table to use was a lovely sight. It gave me a convenient place to cook food, to sit and eat a meal in real comfort and to sort out my things and keep them off the ground. As the tables were nearly always the sort with an attached bench, I could then also turn round and sit and read with my back supported by the table. Real luxury indeed! Enjoying a table like this always reminded me of the verse in Psalm 23, 'You prepare a table before me'; however, in my case, the rest of the verse did not apply as I wasn't 'in the midst of my enemies'!

My pack beside a very welcome table at a campsite in north Wales.

'What do you do to keep in touch?'

By the time I met Jackie, I was also sometimes buying a copy of the *i* newspaper[16], which contained just enough information to keep me informed about the outside world and for me to read in an evening and then throw away or preferably recycle. Early on my walk I had been shocked to learn of the drowning of hundreds of migrants in the Mediterranean. I felt embarrassed when I only found out about this about a week after it happened. The farmer who mentioned it to me in conversation was clearly surprised that I didn't know about this tragic incident. This made me resolve to make more effort to keep in touch. Once I had passed Aberdaron, I found I was passing village shops selling papers quite regularly and buying and reading a newspaper every two or three days became quite a feature of my walk.

I had decided early on in the planning of my pilgrimage to make the trip as low-tech as possible. This fitted in with my own inclination and lack of expertise with technology, but also seemed to be more in accord with the principle of being on a pilgrimage and seeking to spend more time in quiet and with God. On a very practical level, I had a very basic phone, which those with greater knowledge of these things assured me would use relatively little battery charge. Looking back on it now, I was probably being a little overcautious, as I only put my phone on briefly each evening to text my husband to tell him where I was. This was what we had agreed to do.

However, I was often in a place with little or no reception, in which case I often put my phone on again in the morning as I set off walking, especially as I approached higher ground. Then my text could go and I would receive a message from my husband. Even with this frugal use, the charge on my phone got very low at times. On a few occasions I texted him with a 'default' location to meet up a few days later, in case I wasn't able to use my phone at all. A few times I used a phone box (including one with large weeds growing into it), but these

New life for an old phone box in mid Wales.

were often not working or they were in places that were not very useful to me. Keeping my phone charged became quite an issue on my walk. Although many campsites now have pitches with power, these are geared to family camping with a car and you need an outdoor-type adapter to hook up to them. These are bulky and heavy and quite impractical for me to use. My husband had been keen for me to use a small solar charger which he had bought a few years previously. However, this proved useless on all but a few occasions. The sun didn't seem strong enough to power this device, which wasn't designed to be used on the move.

Occasionally I stayed at sites where electricity was available for free and I could charge up my phone indoors, but these were few and far between and running out of battery became quite a concern to me at times. There was not just the issue of the routine text but also the need for power to make an emergency call – which was fortunately never necessary. I have to admit that sometimes, when I was feeling lonely, I would put my phone on just to see if there was a text from Martin. If there was, I would read it several times over. I allowed myself to text my children on a few occasions too, notably their birthdays. I also needed to hear from a friend who was keen to join me but had been uncertain when she would make it.

Otherwise, I had made it quite clear that I was incommunicado. I had told my husband to open any emails for me on his computer at home; it is sobering how few emails of any real import I received. When my husband joined me in the camper van, we would often stay at a site with internet access or we would go to places with wifi on my 'day off'. This enabled me to answer any emails that genuinely needed a response from me.

A few members of my family had found my inaccessibility quite puzzling, but, as I pointed out, anyone was free to come and visit me and indeed to walk with me. Although several people had mentioned that they would like to join me, the practicalities of this were difficult, and only two people apart from my husband actually did so in the end: my eldest son, Chris, joined me for a wonderful day and night, and an old friend, Jane, went to a lot of trouble to join me for a day on the north Wales coast.

My decision to stay low-tech also impacted on the maps I was using, which were the traditional paper Ordnance Survey maps. I simply didn't have the sort of phone that could have stored sufficient maps electronically and even if I had, this would have hugely increased my need for electricity as I would have needed to keep my phone on much of the time and the phone itself would also have had to be more powerful. The maps I used were nearly all 1:25,000 Ordnance Survey maps, although I did use a few 1:50,000 maps that I already had at home[17]. I kept my maps in the van and swapped them over each time my husband visited me. Even so, I generally had three maps with me, which is a considerable weight. On one long stretch when I did not see Martin for two weeks, I had five maps with me, three of which I posted back to him at home. Some of the maps I already had at home as we have quite a collection, some were bought new for the trip and a few I bought en route. I now have a lot of maps of Wales!

'Camping here is my gift to you'

Receiving gifts and offers of help was not something I'd considered before I left on my pilgrimage. I had just thought in terms of being reasonably self-sufficient and travelling light. The lovely words 'Camping here is my gift to you' were spoken by a campsite owner near Porthmadog. I had arrived at his very pleasant and comfortable campsite, which was right on my route. When I arrived, I had got talking with him and his friend about my pilgrimage. They had all sorts of ideas about places I would find interesting and worthwhile and they made various suggestions as to where I could visit. At one point in the conversation his friend asked, 'Is this a Christian pilgrimage? This question encouraged me, because they had made a correct deduction from the details of my walk that I'd mentioned to them, even though I hadn't used such a precise description.

Returning to the practicalities, the site owner was concerned for me and told me not to pitch my tent in his camping field as there would be no one there but me, but to put it up in the main area of the site near occupied caravans and close to the spotless facilities. The kindness of Gerald's words and his concern really impressed me. What a thoughtful gift!

However, I received other gifts and offers of help on many occasions. The first was breakfast, given to me by a kind and curious site owner near Builth Wells. We shared bacon and eggs and coffee together. A week or so later, though, I faced a more serious situation when, after a long and tiring day, the campsite I had been counting on turned out to be just for static caravans and the owner was nowhere in sight. It was late in the day and three or four miles' walk to the nearest village. Someone had told me that if I ever got into difficulties, I should go to a farm and ask to camp. I saw a farm nearby with a caravan in the driveway, and thinking these would be people who knew about needing to find a site, I approached the house. A woman of forty or so and girl of about nine were in the garden, and I told them my story. Within about two minutes, I had the use of their large summerhouse with both a bed and a futon in it and with the heating on. I was then ushered into their house for a meal. They generously opened a bottle of wine for me and later I even got to look through the children's Welsh homework. It was a wonderful evening and was followed by coffee and toast in the morning.

I had a similar experience several weeks later near Holywell. The campsite I had been planning to stay at was small and already full with caravans, and the owner insisted she couldn't manage my tiny tent. Faced with the prospect of walking several miles down a busy main road, a man approached me near the village hall. I could see posters about a folk concert there that evening and people were clearly getting ready for this. When I explained my problem to this man, he told me that it was his family who were putting on the concert that evening and their home was nearby. He invited me to camp in their garden, where one of his sons had already pitched his tent. All I needed to do was go to the concert. These kind people also fed me a meal, and I got to meet the band and the support group. Another wonderful evening!

Another day when I particularly experienced people's kindness was when I was in a small resort near Port Talbot. I'd already had quite lengthy conversation with an older man who had told me a lot about the detective books he had written, and about his family. I thought I had had that day's significant conversation and, knowing that I had quite a long walk ahead of me, I almost tried to avoid any more human contact. But I didn't succeed, as only half a mile or so further on, a man called out to me, saying, 'That looks like a heavy pack.' This led to me offering it to him to try for himself, as I didn't see my pack as really that heavy. He declined this offer but we soon got talking about my pilgrimage, an idea that immediately resonated with Mike and his wife Mary, who said that she too had been on pilgrimage on several occasions.

I was invited back to their home nearby for coffee. As we walked along the road, I saw a house with a beautiful and particularly colourful garden. I remarked on this, a comment which Mike and Mary both seemed to ignore. Then I began to realise that the house in question was their home. Thus began one of the most amazing mornings of my walk. The couple were committed Catholics who had been on pilgrimage to Lourdes and various other places especially important to them. I was somehow drawn into the love and hospitality they offered me. We had coffee, and soon I could hardly believe I had only met them a short time before.

Amongst many other things, we discussed my route and, hearing that I had not visited nearby Neath Abbey, Mary got her keys and said we were going on an outing there. I had noticed this historic site several times from the M4 motorway but had never visited. We drove the twenty minutes or so in the car and arrived at the abbey, now surrounded by busy roads, a small industrial area and a house. It was in the car that Mike and Mary began to talk more about their faith and their lives. Mary had come to faith as a Catholic from a Protestant background. When asked how this happened she just said, 'It was the nuns,' and explained how her husband had grown up in a Catholic orphanage run by wonderful Sisters. Further details of their lives were shared, notably the challenges of supporting their son, who suffered a long-term illness. Returning to their home, I was then given lunch and when I needed to get on my way, they insisted on giving me their phone number in case anything went wrong, implying that that they would come and get me at the end of the day if I needed a bed for the night.

Another remarkable gift I was given was help in retrieving my mobile phone and solar charger. Arriving at a campsite in mid Wales, I realised I didn't have my phone and was certain I had left it and the charger at the previous campsite I'd been at. The weather had been very sunny and I had left my phone and its solar charger propped up on a trailer left in the camping field. In my absent-mindedness, I had walked on that day, leaving them behind. Having arrived at the new campsite, I needed to return to the previous one as fast as I could.

I was near a local tourist attraction with a car park. I ran to try and catch up with a car that appeared to be heading in the direction I needed. Fortunately they were delayed by a passing car, giving me time to get their attention and quickly ask for help. They were the epitome of kindness, driving me some way out of their way to the previous site, where my phone was exactly where I thought I'd left it, and then insisted on driving me back to the new place. At one point they were contacted by phone and I heard one of them say that they were on an errand of mercy, which, in a very minor way, they were. My phone was fine although, ironically, barely charged up at all.

Not all the gifts I was given were particularly substantial. One day, walking into the village of Trawsfynydd, north of Dolgellau, after quite a demanding morning's walk, a man called to me from his Land Rover, asking me what I was doing. I outlined my story, to which he replied 'Do you want an apple?' reaching out with one in his hand. For a very brief moment I thought of refusing, as I already had an apple to eat and I was also confident there was a village shop nearby. But I decided to accept, feeling I could accept a small gift of an apple just as well as a larger gift of a meal or a place to camp.

Later on my walk, whilst walking across Pembrokeshire, I was very relieved to find a campsite in an area where I had not been able to see anywhere to camp when I was researching my walk. As I planned in the months before I set out, I had tried to find a trickle of campsites that I could use. The details of these places were written in my notebook. However, the area I was then in appeared to be lacking sites, perhaps because of the huge popularity of the nearby coastline. As I approached the village, a site appeared alongside the road. Arriving at this quiet – in fact almost deserted – spot, the owner's son-in-law appeared with a cup of tea and a plate of biscuits. I am not normally someone who would photograph a plate of biscuits, but I could not resist this after such a kind gesture. At another site I was also given sandwiches to take for my lunch and at another, a small quantity of milk for my tea: a real treat.

Accepting lifts as a form of gift was something I thought of early on in the pilgrimage. I started out with a very determined policy of not accepting lifts, but this thinking was challenged quite early on in my walk when someone offered me a lift a mile or two up a main road to a campsite that had just been recommended to me. I refused this lift and then spent half an hour or so walking up this quite busy road at the end of what had been quite a long walk. Being on this road and keeping out of the way of the traffic made me realise that I had made a mistake. Not only had I possibly put myself in some danger as it was almost dusk, but the kind lady who offered me a lift seemed snubbed by my refusal of her offer. If I had accepted, I would also have been able to tell her a little of my trip and plans and, indeed, learn a little about her life. I realised I had been wrong.

A few days later a similar situation arose. I was walking along a quiet lane but knew I would need to walk along a busier road to get to the campsite I was heading for. A pick-up truck drew up alongside me; the driver asked me what

I was doing and insisted on giving me a lift. I had learned from my mistake and got in. What followed was a fascinating conversation with a man who was both a farmer and an environmentalist. Although he was keen to offer me space at his farm to camp, this was too far out of my way and he dropped me near the campsite I had in mind. I did later wonder whether I should have accepted his offer, but I would have needed a lift again in the morning to get myself back on track. I did accept lifts on two or three further occasions, but only ever for a mile or two. Not only did it seem churlish to refuse kind offers, but it led to more opportunities to meet and chat with people.

'Why do you have a stick with you? Is it to fend off Welsh farmers?'

I immediately assured the Welsh farmer who asked me this that I had begun to use a walking pole several years before when I was having considerable problems with my right knee. Using a stick seemed to take some of the weight off that side of my body. The stick then became something of a habit, and something I was increasingly grateful for. I had always, even as a child, felt nervous coming down steep slopes and the stick just seemed to give me some reassurance. It was also useful for some extra leverage when going *up* steep hills. It certainly wasn't intended for defensive use, unless you consider brambles and nettles growing across some less-used paths. However, this farmer had raised the issue of my own safety, which was probably one of the things I was asked about most frequently during my walk.

I sometimes commented to people who asked questions about my safety and security that it was animals that worried me far more than potential danger from people. I am extremely nervous about cattle, and also farm dogs. I was reassured when one campsite owner remarked to me that she was the daughter of a dairy farmer and she felt nervous of cattle too.

41

She thought I was quite reasonable to feel anxious about fields of cows. A farmer in mid Wales also stressed to me to be careful of cattle 'especially in Pembrokeshire where there are lots of fields with cows', particularly as the cattle would be outside more once the weather warmed up in the late spring. Both these conversations helped me to see my fear of livestock as not being without justification, if even these experts thought there was some potential danger. This was one of the reasons why, certainly in lowland areas, I tended to use the network of tiny lanes which is such a feature of the Welsh countryside. This helped me to avoid the possibility of my route taking me into fields of cattle. In fact, the only animal that ever charged me was a ram on the Wye Valley Walk. I went through a small field by the river which contained what looked, to me, like a rare breed of sheep. There was a ram, a few ewes and some lambs, which perhaps triggered the defensive behaviour in the ram. Fortunately a few shakes of my walking pole was enough to put him off, as he certainly looked big enough to knock me over if he'd wanted to.

Another potential danger was that from traffic. However, I found that when I walked on roads, the vast majority of drivers slowed down and gave me as wide a berth as possible; in fact I was generally very impressed with the responsible attitude of drivers. I also made a point of praying as I set out each morning and one thing that I always included was a prayer for protection from danger in whatever form.

Another danger that I faced was the risk of falling or tripping, especially in a remote area. Early on my walk I did have two falls. The first was a simple trip over a bramble runner crossing a rather overgrown path above the Wye Valley. Fortunately the ground was soft, as I fell onto my knees and then my face. Perhaps the most worrying thing about this incident was that my glasses fell off and I then fell onto them. My glasses were not broken, but if they had been, I would have been unable to read my map and would have had to suspend my walk until my husband brought me my spare pair of glasses or, indeed, I had been able to make it to a town big enough to have shops that sell reading glasses off the shelf.

In my need to keep down the weight and volume of my kit, I had decided that my spare glasses needed to be in the van but not with me in my pack. I realised that this incident happened when I was feeling tired towards the end of a long day, and that trying to avoid days that were too long for me, or too hilly, was an important consideration. The second fall was a few days later in a more remote area, when I tripped over on a stony path whilst I was preoccupied with looking at the map. Stopping to look at the map rather than trying to multi-task would probably be the lesson of this incident. I quite badly hurt my shins as I fell forward, the pain then being such that I needed to sit down on the (fortunately dry on a warm day) path as the fall had left me feeling quite faint. I could see a few people in the distance working on what was perhaps a new wind farm. It occurred to me that if I had sustained a more serious injury, I could hopefully have got their attention.

As is good walking practice, I had a whistle with me at all times to get attention. I also tried to ensure I had sufficient charge on my mobile phone to call Mountain Rescue. For the first half of my walk I also had a survival blanket with me, which I would consider an essential bit of kit when walking in more remote areas at any time. However, in the context of this walk, when the spring weather was still very cold as soon as the sun went down, I considered this item particularly important. I also had some basic first aid items: a few antiseptic wipes, a few plasters, a bandage and a few paracetamol and Ibuprofen. Fortunately I never needed any of these items, but it is my opinion that if you walk on your own, you need to have a higher level of preparation than if you are with others. Perhaps the main way that I tried to protect myself was simply by my own planning. I am a reasonably competent map-reader and this allowed me to venture safely into areas that would be off-limits if you did not have a decent understanding of maps.

However, what most people had in mind when they expressed

their concern about my safety was probably danger from other people; especially as a lone woman, the danger from men. The fear of violence, and in particular sexual violence, was alluded to by several people I met. I worked on the basis, though, that I was no more likely to fall into this type of danger than in any other type of place or doing any other activity; in fact I expect my risk was lower than in many situations. I also work on the basis that the vast majority of men act benevolently, and indeed chivalrously, most of the time. In fact, the only time I felt threatened was by a young woman at a well-run campsite in a town. When I first arrived at the campsite, she appeared rather silly and had perhaps been drinking. Later I had to shout over to her and her friends to be quiet as they were making considerable noise late at night. When the noise started up again at 2 a.m., I heard her come over to my tent and interfere with my kit in the tiny awning. I warned her sternly that if she didn't leave my things alone, I would go to the police in the morning. I woke early the next day before the site office had opened and did not pursue this incident any further, but it was the only occasion when I felt in any way threatened by another person.

'Do you have money?'

This question was asked by a girl of about seven or eight years of age. She and her little sister asked me a variety of simple and commonsense questions about my trip. I replied that I did have money, just like other grown-ups had. I tried to make sure that I had £30 or so on me, although this was often not the case. The theory was that if I had needed to get bed and breakfast or stay in a hostel, this sum would have been sufficient even if the place didn't take credit or debit cards. In practice, things didn't work out like that: on the only occasion when very bad weather combined with bed and breakfast being available, it cost me £50 for single occupancy of a nice double room. There was also a cashpoint available nearby as it was in a small town on the Ceredigion coast. The only other time when I chose not to camp, I stayed in a hotel in a well-known chain and they took cards.

At the start of my trip I decided to take a few blank cheques, my debit card, a credit card and the cash 'allowance' of £30 I felt was realistic. Generally, this proved good planning. My husband would give me more cash when we met up, to maintain my cash levels. I used cards where I could, including withdrawing money where possible. However, there were a few occasions in village shops when I needed cash but I was required to spend at least £10 to get 'cash back'. £10 would buy quite a lot of food, which I would also then need to carry, so in these situations I usually just went without cash. I never actually ran out of food or money or was at a campsite and unable to pay for it.

The cost of camping also varied enormously and the cost was generally quite unrelated to the quality of the site. Being near the coast and summer arriving seemed to drive up the cost, but I paid £19, the highest cost at any site, at a place where the toilet and shower facilities were in a bunker-type building and CCTV cameras seemed to track your every move. Even though I was far from any permanent structures, the sound of the camp's disco and so on kept me awake into the small hours. Another site I stayed at cost £15 for what could only be described as grim and grubby.

But the majority of sites were quite different to this. Most were very clean and welcoming. I paid as little as £3 for an excellent site, but more regularly £10. However, many great sites charged me £7 or £8, which I thought was a fair price. One site charging this amount even had a heated TV room, as well as immaculate showers with lots of hot water and good facilities for washing up.

To some extent the difference in what I was charged was because some sites had a set price for any tent, or perhaps a set price for any small tent. In many places I would have been charged just the same if there had been two of us. In one site when I mentioned this discrepancy, using a large family tent nearby as my example, the manager then waived any fee. I had already, politely but firmly, pointed out how inadequate the shower facilities were, especially considering I had had to share these with a school group (which seemed odd from a child protection point of view).

Some sites also didn't differentiate between backpackers carrying all their kit and people camping with cars. One site owner, having charged me £10 (early in my trip when it was still very cold and I was the only person at his lonely campsite) remarked how small my tent was once it was up. He was also charging for showers and mean enough to only provide tiny washbasins in the loos. However, I made do with the washbasin in his 'family bathroom'. How this was supposed to be adequate for small children, I don't know. Parents were obviously supposed to keep paying a considerable extra sum for showers. I wouldn't have minded if the site had been full and popular but I was the only person there and the owner lived off the site, meaning I was also very isolated.

Another not-so-good experience was being charged £10 where there were no showers and only a cold water tap at the basin in the rather grubby toilet. The owner told me I might have been charged less at other places, but this was because the other sites weren't insured 'and you never knew what might happen'. Perhaps it wasn't surprising that I was the only person at this site. However, this was a bargain compared to the £15 a farmer in north Wales tried to charge me for a site where there wasn't even a wash basin, just a toilet and a cold water tap in the field – although I didn't know that when I paid. He must have noticed my disquiet, and reduced his charge to £10. The site had a fabulous view over the sea, which was quite an attraction, but I think if I'd known in advance that there wasn't even a wash basin, I wouldn't have stayed. It's not that I needed any extensive facilities. At one or two other very basic sites I stayed at, there was just a loo and a basin with cold water. This was absolutely fine, provided it was reflected in the cost.

My one-woman tent in the heart of mid Wales.

However, there were good moments too; such as at the laid-back site in mid Wales where the owner immediately reduced his already modest charge because I was on foot. His site also had a large open barn with a big rustic table where campers could sit and eat in bad weather. On another occasion I was allowed to camp in the grounds surrounding some historic ruins .This was all for a modest donation of £2 for the local air ambulance which, as the owner of the field insisted, was quite optional. In this case I also had use of a lovely bathroom inside her own home. On this occasion I wrote in my diary, 'Lovely spot; can't get over how I have gone from homeless/site-less backpacker to pitching my tent in the beautiful and peaceful grounds of the abbey'.

When people ask me about my trip, they often assume that I was doing bed and breakfast, but this would actually have been quite impractical and vastly more expensive. Not only would I have had to pay more for the accommodation itself, but I would also have had to buy myself an evening meal out. Three months of doing this would have been very costly; also, perhaps more importantly, it would have changed the whole nature of my trip. Although I wasn't especially aiming to be economical in my spending, neither did I want to feel I was living beyond my means. I was aware that I did have riches, but these were the riches of having the time, health and opportunity to make my pilgrimage: things that many people do not have.

There were a few other minor expenses as I walked, mainly involving buying a few maps and a few small gas cylinders for my little stove. I had spent some money prior to the trip on a couple of essentials and had also provided myself with some supplies of basic food to keep in the van. There was also the 'hidden' expense of fuel for the van on my husband's trips to meet me, and also the higher costs of sites when we stayed together in the van. Overall, I've never worked out the total cost of my trip – perhaps itself a sign that I was spending responsibly and felt I was getting value for money.

'Do you want any salt-marsh lamb?'

On a couple of occasions I was asked about things that were completely impractical. In quite a remote area of Snowdonia, whilst talking with an elderly farmer and obviously carrying a big rucksack, his son suddenly appeared and asked me if I wanted any salt-marsh lamb. This seemed a laughable comment given my usual diet of tins of sardines and chunks of cheese. I simply had no means of cooking or even eating salt-marsh lamb – which he immediately realised as I glanced meaningfully over my shoulder at my pack without saying a word.

On another occasion in south Wales, at a Sunday morning service, I was asked if I would like to join the choir; another nice but impractical suggestion.

'You need to know more about where you're going to stay each night'

This was spoken to me as a rebuke by the owner of a caravan site, who told me she was taking me in even though she didn't have a licence to take tents, because she felt concerned for me as a woman walking on my own. This was at the end of a long day where the campsite I thought I had found in a reliable campsite book turned out not to exist either on the ground or at the end of a phone line. A passing driver had then taken me to this lady's small site, the alternative being walking along a busy road. The caravan site owner was clearly concerned; being an older woman, she said I reminded her of her daughter. Perhaps her comment came partly from maternal instinct. I could see that her reprimand was appropriate. She kindly took me in and this conversation went on over a welcome mug of tea and some fruit cake.

This was towards the end of my pilgrimage and I certainly realised that she was right and that I needed to plan future trips with more care, especially in areas where places to stay were few and far between. Such places were more in the urbanised areas of south Wales; in the north and certainly on the coast, I usually found a place to stay without too much trouble.

One exception to this, however, was in mid Wales, where I had imagined it would be easy to find a campsite but this proved to not be the case. I could have taken the bus to Dolgellau about seven miles away and then returned by bus and resumed my walk in the morning, but I was deterred from this by it being a Saturday and being unsure of what buses might be running the next day, on a Sunday in rural Wales.

I decided to wild camp on a small area of National Trust land close by some public toilets, which appeared to remain open all night. I had tried to find a more remote place, but I couldn't find anything other than fields with livestock or steep and stony paths near a stream.

I had a rather anxious night, worrying about being noticed and moved on. Strictly speaking, wild camping is illegal in Wales (and England) without the permission of the landowner. However, I followed one of the rules of wild camping, which is to pitch late and take the tent down early. I made my meal on a useful picnic table and only when it was getting dark did I put up my tent. There were houses quite close by, but no one seemed to notice. I was on the road by 6 o'clock the following morning, having surprised an early-morning commuter who called in at the Ladies to find me washing at 5.30 a.m.!

Living in faith and trust

I got into a routine of committing each day to God in prayer, using a formula I developed over the first few days. You might even have called this a liturgy.

The items in my prayer were a response to my needs and concerns as I saw them on my pilgrimage, hoping to encourage myself in hope and trust. Like points in many a sermon, the sections of my prayer all began with the same letter: Protection, Peace, Provision, Plans and Purposes.

Often I would pray first for God's protection from any kind of danger – a prayer I would repeat later if I found myself on a busy road, for example. Obviously I had my own plans, but I would then ask God to intervene with His plans if His and mine were not the same. I would also pray that I would be aware, in some small way, of His wider purposes in my life or the lives of those I met and their communities.

I was also very aware that I needed God's peace in my heart, a peace that would come from staying close to Him. I also asked each day for God's provision of what I needed in terms of health and strength, places to visit and rest at along the way and for a good place to stay each night. It occurred to me on my walk that each day was a bit like life. If you're not careful, you can spend lots of time and energy worrying about how things will work out. Then, at the end of the day, you realise that in spite of all your fears, everything has worked out well.

At one campsite, after a long and hilly day, I noted with thankfulness the following things: firstly that the owner had picked me up in his 4 x 4 at the bottom of his long farm track. 'Just put your pack in the back and get in,' he said. I had always wanted someone to say this – it sounded so carefree. Secondly, there was also a small shop at his campsite. There was hardly anything in this shop except a few big bars of mint chocolate. After such a long day, I treated myself to one of these. Together with the lovely showers, what more could I want? Yet I often felt anxious, especially in the afternoons when my tiredness increased and I felt the pressure of finding somewhere to stay. Living in an attitude of faith and trust was a difficult lesson, even though on many occasions I felt quite overwhelmed by God's provision.

CHAPTER 3

'What do you do when you get to these places?'
THE MAIN POINTS OF MY PILGRIMAGE

MY PLAN TO make Holywell, Bardsey, St David's and Llantwit Major the main points of my pilgrimage was built on the idea that I was in some way following in the footsteps of medieval pilgrims. These places are, very roughly, in the 'corners' of Wales, being in the far north-east, the north-west, the south-west and the south-east respectively[18]. These four sites, like many religious sites in Wales, originally emerged in the early medieval period[19]. In fact, all these places have traditions, if not traceable history, that go back to the first two hundred years or so after the Romans left. This was one of the main reasons for my interest in them.

However, it was only later in the medieval period that they became places of pilgrimage in the sense that they preserved the memory of a saint or saints from an age that was already long past. As a historian, I felt I needed to distinguish between the original Christian site and its importance to contemporaries, and the cult of pilgrimage that didn't start until several centuries later. Both these facets interested me, but I felt that I needed to keep them separate in my mind. As a pilgrim myself, I wanted to appreciate both aspects of the history of these significant sites as well as adding something for myself as a twenty-first century Christian. I anticipated spending two or three days in these places rather than the single night I spent almost everywhere else, doing whatever was offered to pilgrims and spending extra time in prayer and quiet. I had also decided to stop for a couple of days at the smaller pilgrimage site of Pennant Melangell, as this was on my route between my home and Holywell. Thus the walk north to Holywell via Pennant Melangell became the first leg of my journey.

As well as taking me between the four main points of my pilgrimage, my walk was also punctuated by changes in terrain and a sense of completing a certain proportion of the journey. I also noticed the differing perceptions of people along the way and their comments on the places I was heading for.

As I set out, I saw Pennant Melangell as my first destination. Chatting with people along the way, few people had heard of the place I was heading for; however, as I got closer, more people recognised the name. When I was at Newtown (*Y Drenewydd*), which is about 25 miles away, I finally met people who had been there and I felt as if my goal was in sight. It was encouraging to be able to note in my diary that day, 'Met two people who have heard of Pennant Melangell'.

A few days after leaving Pennant Melangell, another notable point was seeing the high peaks of Snowdonia for the first time as I walked along the Clwydian Hills in north-east Wales. These high peaks, to my west as I walked, were covered in snow. This made even more of a contrast between them and the more modest hills of mid Wales from which I had come. I also saw the sea for the first time that day, looking over the Menai Strait and the coast of north Wales.

A few days later, another amazing view that took me by surprise with its sheer panorama was that over the Dee Estuary from the hills above Holywell. This view led my eye over the Dee and into northern England, where I could clearly see Liverpool, Manchester and the hills of the Pennines. Further away, I could see what I thought was Pen y Ghent in northern Lancashire and even the southerly peaks of the Lake District.

Meeting up unexpectedly near Holywell with a group of pilgrims heading for St Asaph marked a turning point of a different type, as I then walked across north Wales with them to Aberdaron, and on to the island of Bardsey by boat. In my planning and in my mind I was a solo walker and had not intended to walk in a group. Although walking with them was good fun and certainly added a new dimension to my pilgrimage, it made it impractical to go over to Anglesey, a large island off the coast of north-west Wales, for a few days as I had originally intended. This was because their route did not include the island. Walking on my own again as I left Aberdaron, I went mainly on the coastal path up the Llŷn Peninsula and then inland as far as Blaenau Ffestiniog. At this point I had about half of my pilgrimage behind me, which seemed something of a milestone. I wrote in my diary, 'Am about halfway on my walk/pilgrimage/trek, but seem to have been doing this forever.'

I then walked south on an inland route most of the way to St David's. This was clearly the most well-known place to most of the people I chatted to, which perhaps reflects the considerable network of pilgrim roads and hostels which were available to support the medieval traveller or pilgrim to St David's. The modern and medieval visitor would share great enthusiasm in making their way to this picturesque site with its cathedral tucked away in a small valley.

However, lovely though most of the walking was as I approached this tiny cathedral city, the terrain was clearly changing. On May 25th I wrote, 'It does seem a little sad that apart from some of the coastal path, my route from now on will be relatively busy and I have left behind the higher mountains.'

Having arrived in St David's, I spent one day walking on a particularly beautiful part of the coast path and then cut across north Pembrokeshire, heading for Carmarthen (*Caerfyrddin*). Near there, the western end of the Brecon Beacons came into view, which made me realise how close to home I was getting. This was something of an illusion though, as heading south east to Llantwit Major, I lost my encouraging sight of the Beacons. I had also entered territory that was quite new to me.

I then walked to Cardiff, over to Cwmbran and then up the Usk Valley. Just north of Cwmbran, I moved back onto the first map I had used. Throughout my walk I had almost obsessively highlighted each day's route on my map every evening. As I neared home and resumed using the map I had had at the start of the walk, it was great to complete the circle, not just on the ground but on my precious maps.

Pennant Melangell

As I walked roughly north from my home in the Black Mountains to Holywell in Flintshire, the church at Pennant Melangell, a small but ancient place of pilgrimage, was more or less on my route. This lovely place is in the north of the county of Powys in the Berwyn Hills, in effect in the far south-east corner of Snowdonia. The story behind this site is thought to date back perhaps to the seventh century when Melangell, a young woman who had previously fled from Ireland to escape what we would now call a forced marriage, was found at prayer by a lordly huntsman. The hare which was the object of his and his hounds' pursuit had taken refuge in the folds of Melangell's cloak. The devotion of the woman silenced even the huntsman's horn and he granted her the valley as her own.

Today, the church at Pennant Melangell is a lovely place to visit; close to the end of the long Tanat Valley, steep hills crowd around where Melangell's hermitage may have been and where a nunnery is thought to have been in existence by the eighth century. Inside, it's cluttered with things to see, prayers to say, candles to light and silence to dwell in. It's a soft, almost feminine place where gentleness is espoused: a cross is bedecked with butterflies and a bird's nest, full of coloured eggs, sits at its base. It's a place where you might expect it to be colder inside than out, but on a fine April day, the opposite seemed true. The church felt warm; I even tried, in vain, to find the source of the heating.

There are centuries-old features to admire, including the carefully rebuilt shrine in its muted, pink cover. This, a very early example of the Romanesque style in northern Europe, dates back to the twelfth century. You can leave your prayers under the shrine in a similar way to medieval pilgrims. Melangell herself, in effigy with two hares cuddling up to her side, lies in stone in

55

the sanctuary. Beyond that, a small cell holds what may be her gravestone.

However, the gentleness and devotion that Pennant Melangell encourages belies the fact that this is one of the few ancient church sites in Wales that has been extensively excavated by archaeologists, with associated study of the surviving life of Melangell, the *Historia Divae Monacellae*[20]. Excavations revealed not only early Bronze Age pottery (about 2000 BC) but also remains, including fragments of human bone, indicating that the site had been a place for disposal of material following cremations in the middle Bronze Age (about 1000 BC). There was also evidence of a possible causeway onto the site in the early medieval period, with burials at that time. The evidence also pointed towards an earlier structure of wood and thatch that predated the existing church, which goes back to the twelfth century.

The antiquity of this site is remarkable: perhaps in continuous use, or certainly veneration, from the early Bronze Age into modern times. Relating the archaeological evidence and literary sources to what could be reasonably surmised about Melangell and her presence at this site is a challenge, but not impossible to attempt. The literary sources claim that Melangell was of Irish descent, not improbable given the close links between Ireland and Wales at this time. Pennant Melangell's proximity to an existing burial site also fits in with what we know of the preference of the early saints for places that were already revered in pagan times. What appears to be the use of this site in the early medieval period as a cemetery also supports the view that the places associated with early saints were often places of burial not just for the saint themselves but also for followers or disciples in succeeding generations. Melangell's *Life* also states that she was joined by virgin companions to form a convent, although the physical evidence to support this is very slight (just the depiction of Melangell as an abbess on the church's rood screen[21], which dates to the late fifteenth century), so perhaps this small religious foundation was short-lived. It was certainly no longer in existence by the twelfth century, when the shrine was built to house the relics and provide focus for the cult surrounding Melangell which had grown up by this time. The spiritual attraction of this place has also come into the contemporary world in the existence of a small retreat centre (the Saint Melangell Centre) nearby, which provides a variety of activities for the modern pilgrim.

The story of the hare also provides a wildlife theme to this place, which fits well with twenty-first century concerns over species at risk, hunting and habitat loss. However, Melangell is not the only person recorded as giving sanctuary to a hare fleeing huntsmen. Eadmer's 'Life of Saint Anselm' records how the saint in 1097, whilst Archbishop of Canterbury, also had a frightened hare seek safety between the legs of his horse. In 'Hare Encounters' in *The Hare Book*, a modern take on this is given by a cyclist who had a hare circle him whilst he was on his bike.

Holywell

I arrived at Holywell in late April, too early in the season to take part in any of the regular events for pilgrims, but I still very much appreciated what I *could* do there. I was overjoyed to have achieved the first section of my pilgrimage; I spent considerable time just sitting beside the pool below the well, enjoying the stillness and the prayerful atmosphere of the place. However, at Holywell I was also moved by the sight of the vast quantity of water bubbling up into the well. What an image of the abundant life that God offers us. I also found it especially moving to visit a place which is in Roman Catholic guardianship and is very closely associated with Catholicism. It has survived in spite of considerable persecution by the established church and the state, a history which is told well in the museum on the site ('after 200 years of persecution by Church and State following the Reformation, mass could again be openly said,' was perhaps the most obvious example). The museum also very frankly discusses the difficulty we have as modern people in accepting the miracle of St Winifred's severed head being restored to her body by her uncle St Beuno, this being the miraculous event behind the origin of this site. This story is presented as something we do not need, and are certainly not required, to believe in. The museum texts discuss how what we know of St Beuno suggests that he had a great capacity for empathy and for the healing of the mind; surely modern concerns. In fact the whole story of Winifred, which is one of restoration after a violent sexual assault, is dealt with not only in a refreshing and intellectually honest manner but also in a way that somehow builds faith too.

It was challenging too to see the expectation that some of my fellow pilgrims had as regards receiving God's blessing, if not a miracle, when they bathed in the waters. I had learned a little about this a few days before when visiting an old church in the care of Cadw, the Welsh heritage organisation[22]. I talked for some time with a Cadw staff member who told me that, having had a persistent problem with her foot, she decided to dip it in the waters at Holywell and it got better! I had not really expected such a story when I first got talking with this person about my plans. I was also rather amused to hear that her son saw Holywell as a good place to visit when he had money problems. It was also powerful to see, whilst I was there, a group of travellers arrive to bathe in the waters. It was very cold for the time of year and I very much admired them for getting into the pool; all I did was dip my feet in, thankful that they had carried me so well so far. However, the travellers' enthusiasm was not to be doubted. A young woman and an older man stayed in the pool for some time, repeatedly circling, as is the custom, then dipping under the water and kissing the stone sides. These two did this with such fervour that I found it quite moving. It's easy to overanalyse our faith and, in our intellectual quest for information, forget that this group was probably more similar to a group of medieval pilgrims than I am ever likely be with my notebook and my camera.

The very beautiful well chapel at Holywell dates from the early sixteenth century, although Holywell is known to have been a place of pilgrimage since at least the eleventh century. It enjoyed considerable royal patronage, with Henry V being amongst those who went on pilgrimage there – in his case to give thanks for victory against the French at Agincourt. The buildings seen today predate the Reformation, which would challenge the basis of their existence, by just a few decades: they were probably built in the early 1500s on the orders of Margaret Beaufort, the mother of Henry VII. Pilgrimage to such places as Holywell was contrary to the theology of the Protestant reformers of the sixteenth century, but such was the tradition of pilgrimage to this place that the practice never actually stopped, even during the two centuries or so of oppression of Catholic beliefs and observance in England and Wales.

Perhaps one of the most remarkable things about this place is the huge volume of water that issues from the spring and into the well chapel. This spring was diverted in the early twentieth century, after the original source was reduced as a result of huge quarries being dug on the hills above the site. The water flowing from the well then becomes a river sufficiently large to have powered several sites during the early years of the Industrial Revolution. It makes a short journey to the Dee estuary, where medieval pilgrims were able to arrive by boat, and where the Romans may also have had a wharf.

Intriguingly, there is a tradition that the valley was originally called the Sychnant; that is, the 'dry steam'. This is alluded to in an emotive letter of 1904 from Lady Mostyn, who was a member of a Catholic family well-known in north-east Wales. She wrote to the local newspaper, protesting at the effects of mining around Holywell on 'St Winifred's life-giving stream' and the fear that the valley might 'be returned to its original dryness'. Welsh place names are frequently derived from descriptions of the landscape. This may be clutching at linguistic straws, but if the valley had, long ago, been called the 'dry valley', this might just provide some very slight evidence for there having been a key event in the past when water began to flow from the spring. In 1913 local Catholics again protested at the likely effects of mining on St Winifred's Well, as recorded in the Catholic journal, *The Tablet*.[23]

Bardsey

Bardsey is believed to be the burial place of several of the more notable early saints, such as Deiniol, the first Bishop of Bangor, who was buried there in 584. However, it acquired a reputation as the burial place of thousands of holy men and women of the early medieval period. Hearing of this, I was reminded of the custom still found amongst some Orthodox Christians today of going into a monastery late in life and living the remainder of one's days in seclusion and prayer. Perhaps devout Christians, both lay people and monks, chose to go to Bardsey towards the end of their lives and be buried there? However, this tradition that thousands of early saints were buried there caused the island to become a very considerable place of pilgrimage in the later middle ages. Such was the volume of pilgrim traffic that Clynnog Fawr nearby on the mainland became what we would call a transport hub to cater for all these people.

Christian settlement on the island certainly goes back to the sixth century, when St Cadfan founded a church there. The Celtic *clas*[24] church, a simple form of early monastery, continued into the Norman period. Then it seems to have gone into decline and been taken over by the Augustinians following the rule of St Benedict, one of a few examples in Wales of this sort of continuity between 'Celtic' monasticism and that of Europe as a whole. The rather scant ruins that can be seen today date from the Augustinian period of the monastery.

The island itself shows evidence of settlement going back to the Neolithic period. Today, it is managed by the Bardsey Island Trust and is a National Nature Reserve.

My trip to Bardsey was rather hurried as the quite stormy weather and the tide meant I only managed to be on the island for a few hours. Unlike Holywell, which was quite new to me, I had been to this area many times, visiting the nearby cliffs and gazing over the water to the island. This had been before I reached my teenage years, which perhaps says a lot for the power of memory. Actually going over to Bardsey was a wonderful prospect after so many years, and perhaps a motive behind the whole pilgrimage: at last I had a definite reason and opportunity to go. The weather was doubtful and crossing the rough Bardsey Sound in a small, but powered, boat gave me cause to admire the courage of the early saints and pilgrims who went there in only very small craft.

Although the natural beauty and bleak landscape is striking, with great cliffs and colonies of seabirds, there is little to see there of the spiritual history of the island. Also, you can only stay on the island if you take a room for a whole week.[25] Lovely though this would be, I realised early on in the planning of my trip that I was unlikely to have the freedom to spend that amount of time there.

'Bardsey is a good place for your soul to catch up with your body'

This comment was made to me in the bird hide at Lake Vyrnwy when I got into conversation with a couple after they'd asked about my walk. I was then about three weeks away from actually going to Bardsey. At that point I had never sailed over to the island, although as a child I had seen it many times from the cliffs of the mainland. The lady who spoke these words told me how helpful she had found it to visit Bardsey just for a day, when she and her partner had been having a difficult and busy time in their business. A few days later, I got into another conversation about Bardsey with a woman who ran a lovely small caravan site where I stayed on a very cold night. She, too, had been to Bardsey after a stressful time in her business (this was hard to imagine as the place seemed so peaceful), and had found it helpful to go there. Another Bardsey conversation was with a couple in the churchyard at Clynnog Fawr, who told me that their son had been one of the RSPB wardens on the island.

The island was also the final destination of the pilgrim group I joined as I crossed north Wales, and as we walked it became obvious that reaching it was really important to them. However, only a limited number of seats had been booked to go over to the island, so some people knew that they would have to forego a visit and content themselves with staying in nearby Aberdaron. As I was a 'first-timer', I was kindly allowed one of these places on the boat. Another interesting comment made amongst the pilgrim group as we walked was that Bardsey was something of a spiritual disappointment and that Aberdaron parish church was much more conducive to prayer and reflection. When I had been to both places, I found that this seemed to be true, but I think it may be have been due to the time pressures of visiting an island just for a few hours to fit in with the tides. This tends to make visiting Bardsey something of a race against the clock.

Aberdaron

Although my visit to Bardsey was rather rushed, nearby Aberdaron proved to be an ideal place to relax a little and spend some quiet time on a mini-retreat. This seaside village may seem to consist mainly of rather unpicturesque caravan parks when you approach, but it is well worth exploring. Its industrial heritage (manganese was mined nearby) and the area's magnificent cliffs are almost as much of an attraction as the religious history of pilgrimage and ancient churches. Staying there for a few days gave me the time to unwind a little after a few weeks' strenuous walking. I then spent a day on a mini-retreat, as I intended to do at each of the main points of my pilgrimage. Then, on my final day, I attended a service in the very welcoming local church before resuming my walk.

The local parish church, right by the shore, is an ancient site but was itself probably a successor to an earlier religious community on the higher ground above the village. The church, whose current building dates back to the twelfth century, is quite large, with a double nave. The space has been imaginatively organised to create areas for small groups and a larger Sunday congregation, as well as a bookshop and some displays about the life and poetry of R S Thomas. I spent the best part of an hour just reading about his life and work, which I found very encouraging; I realised I needed to find out more about this man and his bleak but inspiring poetry. There were various prompts to prayer around the church. I also found it encouraging to browse the interesting books in the church bookshop, and to find out that there was a hermit attached, so to speak, to the congregation. I knew nothing of this and was fascinated to find out that someone could live as a hermit in modern Britain.

Aberdaron made a great impression on me. In my diary, I wrote, 'Riches, riches, riches. Am almost overwhelmed.'

Mini-retreats

For several years now, I've tried to spend time in mini-retreats that I organise for myself. I've given these the name 'mini-retreat' because they're never longer than a day.

When I first planned my pilgrimage, I decided to have such a time at each key point of my walk. Spending time in this way, even for just a few hours, can seem something of a daunting prospect, so I've found it useful to plan in advance some sort of 'menu' for the day. My time at St Hywyn's was organised in this way and, having briefly visited the church the day before, I knew that it contained all sorts of resources that would be helpful to me. My 'menu' for that day was as follows:

- to pray for my husband and children
- to pray for my fellow pilgrims as we dispersed after walking across north Wales
- to do the activities in the church that acted as prompts for prayer
- to pray for the ministry there by making a prayer journey around the church
- to spend time in silence

As you can see, this time was fairly structured, which I think is what most of us need. On a very practical note, I intended these plans to keep me occupied on my mini-retreat for perhaps four or five hours.

Often, when planning these times, I will include some Bible reading and perhaps reading morning or evening prayer from the service book. I might also join in with services or other activities at the church in question, although that was not the case at St Hywyn's that day.

However, my day did contain some surprises. Perhaps without thinking, I'd imagined I would have the church more or less to myself. However, there was nearly always also someone else there. Amongst quite a considerable number of visitors, at one point a parent and several children came into the church and then wrote in the visitors' book. It was lovely to then read the children's thoughtful comments and to pray for them and their family. The silence also was different to what I'd been expecting. Even during the times when I was alone in the church, it was never truly silent because there was the constant sound of the wind and the sea. It is just a lovely seaside church! In fact, I ended the day by spending some time on the beach just beyond the churchyard.

Reflections at St David's

St David's was another place that I already knew; in fact it was the most familiar of all the places I visited on my pilgrimage. I had been there many times since my early teenage years and I associated it with my first awareness of spiritual life, a life I barely understood at the time but one that now increasingly makes sense.

Whilst I was there this time I had the opportunity to go to several services at the cathedral, which I very much appreciated. I also was able to spend several hours just sitting in the cathedral, enjoying the atmosphere there and praying for the many visitors. I could see that these included old and young, men, women and children, disabled people, people who were clearly foreigners. One group that caught my eye was a class of older children being given a special guided tour. It struck me how useful and appropriate this was, being expertly given by a member of the cathedral staff. The building and its contents came alive with relevance to the young. Perhaps one reason why I enjoyed seeing all the visitors was that I had often been a visitor myself; in fact perhaps no other place more represents the yearnings, then unrealised, of my younger self.

As at Aberdaron and Holywell, I also listed and prayed for those whom I'd met in the section of the walk I'd just completed; something which seemed especially significant as from then on I was walking roughly in the direction of home.

Llantwit Major

At Llantwit Major I was back in totally unfamiliar territory, never having visited before and knowing little of the local area. Llantwit Major was also different to the other three main points on my walk in that it was never a place of pilgrimage in the conventional sense but, instead, an early and very remarkable Christian centre of learning. Being there reminded me of the importance of study and of my own need for learning. It was wonderful just to admire the collection of ancient inscribed stones associated with the church. These are now housed in a special small museum created for them in what had been a ruined chapel; I was glad just to gaze on the stones. Inspiring too was an artist's impression of what Llantwit Major may have looked like in the early eleventh century; a time when it was already 500 years old[26].

Llantwit Major is a remarkable place with roots back into the Roman period, but is especially associated with St Illtud, from whom the name of the town is derived. Illtud was a very dynamic character of the early medieval period and associated with other notable saints such as St David, St Patrick and St Samson of Dol in Brittany. Samson was a pupil of Illtud and when his *Life* was written by a Breton monk only about seventy years after Illtud's death, considerable information about his mentor Illtud was also included. This has provided some insight into Illtud and his school at Llantwit Major, a place that in today's terms would be a college or seminary.

So although Llantwit Major was one of the four major points of my pilgrimage, it was not a place of pilgrimage in the ordinary sense. It was founded by Illtud in about the year 500 and became a significant place of education for missionary monks in the early medieval period. It has even been described as 'a fifth-century university and Britain's oldest centre of learning'[27]. Illtud himself was closely connected with Brittany, even being considered Breton by some, and the monks who lived and studied at Llantwit Major frequently also went to live and work in the English West Country and over in what is now France. It is thought that thousands of monks may have trained here, until the time of Viking raids in the tenth century when the monastery seems to have been severely curtailed in its activities.

The church that can be seen there today falls into three sections. There is the church itself in the east part of the building, and the beautifully restored former chantry chapel at the west end (now a museum for the church's collection of ancient inscribed stones). However, the large middle section of the building, known as the Galilee Chapel, is believed to be on the site of the original foundation of St Illtud.

On my pilgrimage I visited three other churches dedicated to St Illtud, the first being at Llanelltyd near Dolgellau, which was unfortunately locked when I visited rather early in the morning. However, this site is the only one dedicated to St Illtud in north Wales: he is very much a saint of the south. The next church dedicated to him that I came across was at Pembrey *(Pen-bre)* near Llanelli, where there was some useful information about how the early saints may have built up a circuit of embryonic churches by visiting places over time to preach, convert and baptise. This may explain why saints' dedications tend to be clustered in particular areas. The other St Illtud church I visited was at Mamhilad *(Mamheilad)* near Pontypool, not far from my home, on the eastern edge of his range.

CHAPTER 4

'I decided to go somewhere other than a graveyard'
ON BEING A CHURCH VISITOR

THIS WAS THE comment of a man, perhaps in his late thirties, that I got talking to just outside the door of the parish church in Aberdaron. Together with his girlfriend, we must have talked for the best part of half an hour or so, mainly about my pilgrimage. He explained that they had been sitting on one of the benches outside the church but had decided 'to go somewhere other than a graveyard'. They had almost bumped into me as I came out of the church. He considered it very amusing that having wanted to get away from somewhere he associated with death, he should then meet someone doing a pilgrimage.

Churches with a ministry to visitors
Being on pilgrimage made me something of a professional church visitor, a role that I very much enjoyed. It was clear to see that many churches took their ministry to visitors very seriously.

Some of the churches I visited were on the route of church tours in what could be called faith tourism, such as the Sacred Stones trail in Pembrokeshire and the Living Stones heritage route in the Lake Vyrnwy area.

In these cases a group of churches in a locality had got together, often with the help of the local Tourist Board, to encourage people to visit their churches, usually with a focus on interesting features and historic artefacts. These churches had often collaborated to produce informative leaflets or displayed distinctive 'Welcome' signs. One church I visited even had well-designed information plaques in the churchyard to explain key features, and an exhibition area inside.

An interesting variation on faith tourism was a display at the Rug Chapel near Corwen in north Wales. This chapel is an estate church in the care of Cadw, the Welsh Heritage organisation. As well as being a worthwhile place to visit as a beautiful example of a private chapel associated with a landed family, there is also an exhibition about how changing patterns of worship are reflected in church architecture and features. As I looked at this exhibition, I wondered about how many Christians or churchgoers would be able to explain these developments as well as Cadw.

Several churches that I visited also contained small museums of ancient incised stones. The stones contained in these museums are all fascinating, although the museums themselves vary greatly. At Margam Abbey there is an extensive collection in the care of Cadw, contained in a building on the edge of the churchyard. At Llantwit Major, not far away, the church's collection of ancient stones is displayed in the recently restored former chapel at the west end of the church. Also in the Vale of Glamorgan, at Merthyr Mawr, there is a small collection under a shelter in the churchyard. In mid Wales, at Llanbadarn Fawr, there is a small museum inside the church.

However, churches are more than just a collection of historic features and artefacts, and many that I visited made a deliberate attempt to spiritually prompt and challenge the visitor. Many had areas set aside for personal prayer, sometimes with candles to light, a prayer tree to add to, or written prayers available to use and sometimes to take away.

Some churches, too, seemed to be aiming to bridge the gap between offering a spiritual space and the opportunity to visit a historic building by offering a 'peaceful place', where overbusy people can enjoy tranquil surroundings. In mid Wales I came across a group of churches branded as 'Peaceful places'.

Many churches offered informative booklets about the history of their building and its congregation. A few, notably St James' in

Wick (*Y Wig*) in the Vale of Glamorgan, produced a comprehensive guide to the church aimed not only at tourists and pilgrims but also those who might be considering making it their place of worship.

Visiting churches obviously involves the issue of whether those churches are open. People have often asked me since my pilgrimage about whether I found churches open or not. I have to say that the Church in Wales churches I visited generally were open, whereas the chapels and Roman Catholic churches, the latter of which were few and far between, were nearly always closed.

In one church porch I was interested to see an informative poster, produced by an insurance company, claiming that churches were more secure if they were left open, as the local community was more likely to 'own' the building and care for it. It was claimed that insurance premiums would not be any higher if it was decided to leave a church open during the day[28].

On a more mundane level, I visited three churches where there was a tea tray for visitors to help themselves to tea and coffee. In one case, squash and biscuits were provided too.

Church hospitality in the Vale of Glamorgan, south Wales.

'Free and unappropriated forever'

On my pilgrimage, one recurring theme was the use of pews and chairs in different arrangements and to different effects within the churches I visited. I saw churches, such as at Disserth near Llandrindod Wells (*Llandrindod*) in Powys, where the whole of the nave was completely taken up with eighteenth-century box pews, in this case with the name of those who had paid for them still on the door of the pew. In another church, at Llanfaelrhys near Aberdaron on the Llŷn Peninsula, there were box pews down one side and simple benches for the less well-off down the other side, a reminder of nineteenth-century social divisions. I also visited an old Methodist chapel in what was only ever a small village, with tiered ranks of pews enabling hundreds to attend and everybody to see the preacher. In contrast, visiting an Orthodox church in Blaenau Ffestiniog that had previously been a Church in Wales building, I saw that all the old pews had been taken out to create an open space similar to that which would have been the norm in churches in Wales until a few hundred years ago. I also, for the first time, visited a church where in the pews towards the back there were notices asking people to 'Please sit closer to the front'!

However, it was in a small church near Holywell in Flintshire that I saw the most apt notice as regards seats in church. The simple building had been provided by a benefactor in the mid-nineteenth century after the large quarries of the area had isolated the quarry workers and their families from the existing parish church. A notice dating back to when the church was new declared that the seats were 'to be free and unappropriated forever'. These words and the pews to which they referred provide a wonderful symbol of the salvation Christ freely offers us, of God calling each one of us to be His child, and of the fact that the relationship we have with Him has already begun, enduring into eternity. So let's sit on our own free and everlasting seats!

Rood screens

Whilst at the beautiful church at Mwnt in Ceredigion[29], I got into a conversation with two other visitors about the fragments of a medieval rood screen that can be seen in the church. These people told me that they hadn't any idea what this 'rood screen' was (the surviving sections and information in the church didn't give much away). The word that came into my mind at that moment was 'partition', which is perhaps rather a clumsy word with connotations of open-plan offices and so on. However, in late medieval parish churches this partition was between the chancel (where the altar would be) and the nave, which is the main body of the church where the people would stand[30]. The 'rood' itself was the central crucifix raised high above the structure.

Several churches that I visited are well known for their rood screens; in fact I saw some of the best examples in Wales. One of these screens is at Llananno, where the small church is now beside a busy, fast but rural road. The screen is mentioned by R S Thomas, who wrote about his visits to the church in his poem 'Llananno'. He describes the screen as having 'nothing to hide' because there is 'no intermediary between me and God'.

This was one of the issues that the Protestant reformers had with screens. They complained that a screen hid the rite of Holy Communion or the Mass from the worshippers, and had the effect of elevating the role of the priest to that of intermediary between God and man.

Rood screens were also rich in imagery and often contained images of saints and Biblical characters. It was this 'idolatrous' nature of rood screens that first attracted the attention of Protestant reformers in the sixteenth century when the images and crucifixes were nearly all removed from these structures. Any remaining images and sometimes the screen itself were often destroyed under the influence of Puritan thinking in the seventeenth century. However, some did survive – the Llananno screen is exceptional as it also outlived the medieval church, which was demolished in Victorian times, and was reinstated in the rebuilt church. A few miles up the road, at Llanbadarn Fynydd, just a single horizontal beam survives in the church.

I also saw the beautiful rood screens at Patricio and Bettws Newydd on the first and last days of my pilgrimage respectively, both being near my home. Both of these screens date from the late fifteenth or very early sixteenth century, and so were made on the eve of the Reformation. They too are remarkable survivors. What is especially interesting is that it can be clearly seen in both these churches that their screens were three-dimensional structures and that the term 'screen', or indeed 'partition', does not really do them justice.

At the sides of both screens can be seen the stairs giving access to the loft, which is above the lower section of the screen. This provided considerable extra space in medieval churches, allowing worshippers to touch the foot of the rood, and was a place for additional images of saints, for flowers and greenery and for lights. The Bettws Newydd screen is also unique in that the panelling of the rear of the screen, the tympanum, is still intact and goes up to the barrel-vaulted ceiling.

Rood screen in Bettws Newydd, Monmouthshire.

'The screen has nothing to hide'

If you look with fresh eyes at the screens at Patricio, Llananno or Bettws Newydd, you can see that they would only ever have partially kept the people in the nave from looking through: there are plenty of gaps through which they, and we, can gaze. Perhaps we have too readily accepted the view, passed down by those Puritans centuries ago, of rood screens as barriers to a relationship with God. They may have had the opposite effect, of drawing people in to a sense of God's presence, as our eyes are drawn to a window. We can, indeed, come before God as if 'face to face with no intermediary'.

Upkeep of churchyards

When I visited the church at Maentwrog near Porthmadog, I saw an interesting notice about the upkeep of the churchyard. It pointed out that in Wales, the care of churchyards remains the responsibility of the church even after the graveyard is full. Apparently in England graveyards that are full become the responsibility of the local authority. The notice asked relatives of those buried in the graveyard to consider giving money towards the upkeep or to contribute by giving practical help. This seemed a positive response to what must be quite a burden for some congregations.

I noticed that this church also had a very smart toilet, built onto the church but accessible and open to the outside. It was clearly quite recently built and had been designed to blend in well with its historic setting. Clearly a useful amenity for church events and visitors to the graveyard, and the only parish church on my pilgrimage where there was a toilet available for visitors to use.

Take my life and let it be

Whilst walking along the coastal path on the beautiful estuary near Porthmadog, I had the wonderful experience of gradually hearing a lovely sound. Then I realised that not only could I hear a voice singing, but that the voice was singing the well-known hymn 'Take my life and let it be'. There was also the

Visitors welcome at Llanwddyn in mid Wales.

sound of organ music. It was certainly very moving to be walking along in such a place and then so unexpectedly to hear almost mystical singing. As I gradually became aware of the sound, it was also difficult to work out where it was coming from.

Determined to find the source of the music, I walked off the coastal path and realised that it was coming from a church nearby. I had difficulty finding the door of the church; when I eventually got inside, I expected to see least two people.

However, it was just the organist both playing and singing. It was wonderful to listen for a while; I deliberately moved to where he could see me so I wasn't just eavesdropping. It turned out he was practising for a wedding.

First World War memorials

Almost all parish churches contain memorials to those who have died in war. As I walked, I came across two particularly poignant memorials to young men killed in the First World War. The first one, to a nineteen year old, was in the parish church in Ruthin (*Rhuthun*) in Flintshire and took the form of a painting of the three women coming to the tomb of Jesus on Easter morning. The lovely picture, painted by one of the sisters of the dead man, shows the women dressed in the clothes of the early 1920s.

The second memorial, in this case a stained glass window, is in the parish church at Roch in Pembrokeshire. It commemorates the deaths of the two sons of the local squire, one of whom, Roland Philipps, was a leading light in the early years of the Scout movement. Based on a painting, it shows Christ the Pathfinder beckoning a young scout. The window incorporates two pathfinding symbols, one meaning 'I have passed this way' and the other 'Gone home'.

Faithfulness in ministry

In one church that I visited there was a stained glass window in memory of a previous vicar of the parish. This was unlike anything else I have ever seen in that it took the form of three panels showing a clergyman baptising a child, conducting a wedding and celebrating the Eucharist. What a wonderful picture of faithfulness in ministry!

'I love Matins; it wraps itself around you'

Of course, I was also visiting churches as a worshipper, and the comment above was made to me by an older lady who kindly offered me a short lift in her car after a church service near Barry (*Y Barri*). The tiny church was situated in what was hardly even a hamlet. The service, which was surprisingly well-attended, had not in fact been a service of Matins but of Holy Communion.

As on the previous Sundays during my pilgrimage, I prayed that God would lead me to the right church, where I could worship and be encouraged and hopefully be an encouragement to others. The comment about Matins interested me because this very traditional service (the Anglican liturgy dates from 1662) had recently been reintroduced at my home church to, perhaps, a mixed reception. I was quite prepared to give it a go, but I could see that the rather wordy liturgy with its archaic language was not something that everyone would find helpful. As a result, I was fascinated by this comment, made quite out of the blue. It certainly made me think that I needed to keep a more open mind as to whether people, including myself, might grow to love Matins and find it beneficial.

I really appreciated worshipping in a wide variety of churches on the Sunday mornings as I walked around Wales. Some were small village churches, some town churches and a few city churches or cathedrals. I took part in traditional and more contemporary worship. On all these occasions except one, I was warmly greeted and made to feel welcome, and at the city church where there was no welcome, I had the experience of being able to welcome others: two Chinese visitors who needed some help with following the service. Although I found the unfriendliness a struggle at this church, I was pleased to be able to assist the young man, who was studying here in Britain, and his mother, who was visiting him from China. The young man told me that he wasn't a Christian but his mother was. Although it was discouraging not to be welcomed (I did try to get into conversation with the organist after the service, but he seemed to be in a hurry), I was pleased that I could be of assistance to my fellow travellers. This may sound self-serving, but I was surprised that not even one of the sidespeople thanked me for helping the Chinese pair, when it was fairly obvious I had moved seat to sit next to them part way through the service and stayed with them to the end.

However, this was the only such experience that I had in all the Sundays I was away (the first two Sundays I was away, my husband drove me back to our own local church for important services). Across north Wales it wasn't practical to go to church on Sundays, so I only visited nine churches for a Sunday service whilst I was away, and two of these were different churches in the same group on the same Sunday. Apart from at the one service mentioned above, I was very warmly received and I found the experience of worshipping in these different places very encouraging and uplifting. One or two churches stand out in my mind, though, for good reasons rather than not so good. I arrived at one church in my waterproof trousers, having walked up on a very wet morning from the rather grim local campsite (the only site on my whole walk where I had been concerned about the security of my belongings). I had seen several churches marked on the local OS map as being a mile or so away in this suburban area. Trudging up the road in the rain hoping to find a church service about to start, I noticed a rather dull-looking building and as I approached, I could hear music and singing. As I settled myself down near the back in my wet clothes (and began to peel off the outer layer), I was almost overwhelmed by the gentle and meaningful worship. I was moved to tears. The quite large congregation, in what was quite a workaday area, contained a genuine mix of ages and of men, women and children. There was a quite tangible sense of God at work amongst them. Afterwards I was kindly looked after and ushered into their church hall for cake left over from a tea they had held the previous afternoon. This seemed to be something of a 'Feeding of the Five Thousand' situation, as far more people had turned up to this evangelistic and community event than they'd expected and yet they still had lots of cake left. People kindly asked about my pilgrimage and shared something of their lives with me. I felt guilty leaving and regretted that I needed to go. It even occurred to me that perhaps I was meant to stay there for a while, perhaps even permanently – the only time I felt this while on my pilgrimage.

CHAPTER 5

'It must be all the people you meet'
PEOPLE ALONG THE WAY

AT ONE LARGE campsite, I got talking to a man who said he was really glad to have met me. I felt very humbled to have him say this; *I felt really glad to have met him*. Also, on a rare night when I didn't camp, I got talking to a hotel receptionist who asked me about the benefits of my walk, adding, 'It must be all the people you meet'.

When I reached the main points of my pilgrimage, I made a list of all those people who had been a particular help to me and prayed for them as part of my mini-retreat. When I finally got home, I read through all my diaries and made a list of all those people with whom I'd had a significant conversation. The list ran to over 150 names.

'You have these conversations *because* you're on your own'
This observation was made by an Orthodox priest I was visiting in Snowdonia. I had been aware of this man and the Orthodox church he had founded for several years. The presence in my family of several Orthodox Christians had meant that I knew of him and was curious to meet him and to discuss my pilgrimage with him. I realised that I was approximately at the mid-point of my walk, so I felt ready perhaps to reflect on my experiences thus far. Having visited his church, complete with Welsh icons, and the lovely chapel within his own home, we sat down to chat. Like me, he had some time before been a teacher of Religious Education, which gave us several things to talk about. Having been received into the Orthodox Church, he had returned to his native Wales. His church is

one of only a few Orthodox churches in Wales, serving people from the historic Orthodox countries and also some converts. Although he had not seen her for some time, he knew my stepmother, which was a lovely point of contact.

However, it was when our conversation turned to my pilgrimage, and the fact that I was walking on my own, that our talk became the most interesting. Most people were surprised or even shocked that I was walking on my own, but the priest never seemed to question it. I shared with him some of the conversations that I'd had, and that I prayed for a significant conversation each day. We talked about the dynamics of walking on your own and how this 'invites' people to start a conversation. He said that he was also often walking about on his own and had had the same experience. I also described how, when walking across north Wales with the pilgrim group from St Asaph, I had had no conversations of any significance with people outside the group. All our conversation was focussed on ourselves, which, eventually, I found disappointing. Encouraging though it was to walk with them for a while, two weeks was sufficient and I was glad to go back to being alone.

'Do you know where this church is?' (holding up an old photograph)

It often seems to be the case that when you're a stranger in an area, you get asked for directions or to help out with local knowledge. This was exactly my experience when, in the hills of mid Wales, a man lowered his car window on a lane which was little more than a track. He held up a photo of a church that looked like it could be almost anywhere, and asked if I recognised it. He explained that he had taken the photo about twenty years previously whilst working in that area for the electricity company. He hadn't had time to visit the church but had managed to take a photo of the exterior, which he had obviously kept safe all this time. I had to admit to him that I had no idea, although having told him I was on a pilgrimage and visiting old churches, I did feel rather useless. But nearby some builders were working on an old chapel; we approached them and they were able to direct the man with the photo to an elderly local person whom they felt sure would be able to help. The man's quest to find this church really touched me. I clearly couldn't answer his question but I prayed for him as I walked on: that he would not only find the church that meant so much to him, but that he would find much more; the God who is worshipped at that church and who draws us all to Himself if only we will let Him.

This man with his photo was looking for a church and hadn't been able to find it, but on the previous day I had actually also been involved in a very different kind of 'Lost and Found' situation. I was amused that these episodes had occurred on consecutive days.

I had been walking over the Black Mountains on only my second day; in glorious sunshine, I was walking on a quiet track up a steep hillside. I got distracted by a small piece of litter near the path. Despairing of finding rubbish even in this idyllic spot, I bent down to pick it up and noticed another bit nearby. Picking this up, I saw it was a pristine £50 note! I suppose there must have been a previous time when I was in possession of note of such value, but I couldn't recall one. And now, here I was with a £50 note in such extraordinary circumstances.

I carried on up the track and came to a more level place where the river went through some little cascades. Here was a young family enjoying a picnic and a group of young people doing their Duke of Edinburgh Awards who had been at the same campsite as me the previous night. I approached both groups, to explain my situation and to discreetly ask whether the note could be theirs. With both groups, the response was the same: it couldn't possibly be theirs as they just didn't have £50 notes! I carried on, thinking I might be able to hand over the note if I saw a police car – probably a one in a thousand chance in this area.

I still had the note with me when I arrived two days later at the lonely and very beautiful church where I had arranged to meet my husband at the end of my first week. I considered putting the money in the offering box at the church but was concerned that the money was not yet mine to give away. My husband later had the opportunity to take it into our local police station, where it was accepted as genuine; it had crossed my mind that it may be a forgery, especially as it looked very much 'hot off the press'. He was told that the note could be collected in a few weeks if it was not claimed, which proved to be the case.

I often thought at that time about the circumstances in which it had been lost and in which I had found it. The dry and pristine state of the note meant that it must have been lost earlier that morning, but by whom? I was there quite early and for the rest of the day I saw no one apart from the young family and the Duke of Edinburgh group. Eventually we donated the money to the appeal following the then recent terrible earthquake in Nepal.

'We're not sad'

Not all of the people I talked with on my pilgrimage were in straightforward or easy circumstances. Early on my walk I met an older couple and their son, a man of forty or so. They were eating a rather delicious-looking picnic when they asked me to sit down with them on some benches near a beautiful church on a remote hillside. My own rather crumpled sandwich looked rather frugal in comparison. They offered me some lovely homemade apple pie; a real treat for me. I then asked them why they were there.

As they told me something of their story, my own life and its concerns seemed very trivial. Their daughter, the sister of the younger man with them, was buried in the churchyard. In spite of their sad loss, they said they were grateful for such a lovely final resting place for her. That day would have been their daughter's birthday; each year they celebrated her life with a picnic at this wonderful place.

They kindly asked me about my life and what I was doing.

By a coincidence, some of their early memories of their daughter were of her at a place I also knew well. There were lots of questions I would have liked to ask them, but I felt I had to content myself with what information they offered me. The magnitude of what had happened to them and my sharing of their memories in this very tiny way was almost overwhelming. As I got up to leave, I said that I felt privileged to have shared this time with them on what must have been a sad day, to which they immediately replied that they were not sad. Although they didn't expand on this, they seem to have reached a place of peace about their daughter's life and their bereavement.

Later on my pilgrimage, another couple shared with me the seriousness of their son's situation. He had suffered with depression and long-term illnesses for much of his life. 'I don't think he's ever had a friend,' said his mother. He had struggled through school and then managed a few short-term jobs, but his difficulties were so great that he had not been able to cope with living independently. They had had to visit him and support him so much that they had eventually asked him to come back to their home and live with them. The father seemed almost embarrassed that they had a son, in his forties, at home with them; a situation that was very unlikely to change.

I felt very privileged to be able to listen to these and other stories that people told me about their lives. What could I do but commit these people to God and pray that they would somehow know comfort and support in their different situations? This has often been a rather helpless prayer that I have uttered. I may not know what to do, or it may be impractical to offer to help, but I have asked God to send people to give comfort and assistance when I feel powerless to do anything.

A few weeks later, I met someone who was receiving unexpected support from his local church. He explained that he hadn't been a churchgoer but that when his partner had died just a few weeks before, he had visited the local vicar to arrange the funeral. He spoke movingly about how, even though the funeral had only been attended by three people, it had been a wonderful celebration of her life and how much he felt the local vicar cared about his situation. As a result he had started attending church in this rather shabby suburb of a larger town, where I met him one Sunday morning.

After the service, I was kindly invited to have coffee and cake (it was the church where they had held the neighbourhood tea the day before) and got talking with others in the congregation. One woman told me about her grief at losing a grandchild a few years earlier and how this tragedy had resulted in her daughter, the child's mother, losing her faith as a Christian. Another older lady told me her husband had died just a few weeks before. In fact, this group of people, so kind in their sadness, seemed to contain so much heartbreak between them. As I got organised to leave, one of them even said that where I was going, 'You'll find people more interesting than us.' I told them, perhaps rather lamely, that I would pray for them.

However, experiences like these made me wonder whether I should be bolder and pray for people there and then. Although I did grow more open about sharing my faith during my walk and certainly prayed fervently and as best I could after meeting people with such obvious needs, I never actually prayed with anyone.

Praying for other people

As I've said, I never offered to pray with people on my walk, although on a few occasions I said I would pray for them or their situation later. However, there were times when I dearly wanted to pray for people there and then, but perhaps lacking courage, didn't do so. There are probably lots of reasons for this. Some are good reasons, such as being concerned that not knowing much about a person might lead me to say something inappropriate. Some are not such good reasons, like fear of rejection if the person said they didn't want to be prayed for. On one occasion on my walk I went into a small shop to buy a newspaper. Although there was space for newspapers to be set out in the shop, there was just a pile of them on the counter. The lady running the shop said she had been too ill that day to put the newspapers out in the usual place. She clearly was unwell and told me some of her symptoms, which sounded genuinely serious. She told me she had a doctor's appointment later in the day and had already been told she might be sent to hospital. And I was somebody who had just walked through the door and into her shop! Until it became obvious that she did have family around, I was actually considering whether I should stay around and offer to go with her to hospital. She was probably the first person that I met on my walk that I felt I should have offered to pray with. But there's always the fear of being seen as exploiting those who are feeling weak and vulnerable.

Another type of situation occurred when I met a woman whose son-in-law had been killed in a road accident after spending a lot of time serving in the army overseas. This had led to a whole series of situations in which this woman and her family had been let down. I noted in my diary at the time that I didn't know what to pray for as regards the difficulties she faced. It seemed to me at the time that she needed to become more aware of God's love and God's image in others, and also perhaps she needed comfort as she seemed to carry a lot of grief, but who was I to judge her in such a painful situation?

'Have you got a blog?'

Visiting a church for the service one Sunday morning, I was asked by a young woman whether I was writing a blog. When I said I wasn't, she seemed surprised and perhaps disappointed in me. I tried to convey to her that, for a variety of reasons, I had planned for my pilgrimage to be reasonably low-tech. She still seemed unconvinced, to the point where I have to admit that I felt slightly irritated; however, her question made me think through just why what she had considered to be normal had not seemed a good idea to me. Later that day I thought through how writing a blog would have affected the very nature of my walk. It would have required much greater access to electricity and would also have made demands on my rather feeble technical abilities. More significantly, the conversations I had with people were private and not appropriate at all for a blog. It would simply have been a betrayal of trust in many cases, and not something I would have been comfortable with at all. I could have limited my blog to just factual details of my journey but that would have left out what was one of the most interesting aspects of my walk. All in all, I was very happy to write my diary in an old-fashioned notebook each evening. I am still aware of the privacy issue, though, and as I write, I'm careful to ensure that no one could be identified from what I've committed to paper here. There was also the question of the immediacy of a blog, whereas I was trying to achieve thoughtful reflection, something that nearly always requires time.

'Is this café cheap or expensive?'

When I was walking across north Wales, I heard someone I met speak very disparagingly of a town I was intending to visit later on my walk. 'The armpit of Wales' were his words – words that stayed in my mind. A few weeks later, as I approached the town in question, I went into a café for a coffee and got talking to a couple, hoping they would be able give me directions to a church I wanted to visit there. When they'd explained where I needed to go, they beamed at me and, quite unprompted, said how much they loved living in that town. I felt their cheerfulness was quite an antidote to the original comment I'd heard; in fact, I had a brilliant day in the 'armpit' town.

On another occasion I got talking with a man out walking his dog. He looked very run-down; working in heavy industry had robbed him of health, and yet he loved Wales and wanted to tell me about lots of places I could visit. Further on when having a coffee outside a café in a Valleys town, a woman came up to me and just asked, 'Is this café cheap or expensive?' I was pleased to be able to say that their prices were a real bargain, and this seemed to persuade the woman to come and sit next to me; a tale of repeated failed relationships and children taken into care then unfolded.

At another place, I stayed in a huge campsite that seemed

more like a shanty town than a place for a holiday. A man walking his dog came up to me and told me it was easier to care for his disabled wife living in a touring caravan at this site than it was at their 'real' home. Due to some strange legal quirk, you could live all year in a touring caravan whereas the residential vans could only be lived in for part of the year. This place was a real eye-opener into the lives of people who seemed to be living in caravans rather than ordinary houses; I did wonder if some of these people would otherwise be homeless. On another occasion I was lent a phone by a young woman outside a shop. When I asked her name, she spoke a word I had never heard of; she then explained that she thought her mother had meant to call her 'Caroline' but had got confused over the spelling. Needless to say, the name was rather lovely.

We get lots of opportunities to think, 'What would Jesus do?' Would Jesus write off the scruffy, the unpicturesque or the uneducated, whether they be people or places?

Faithfulness in small things

One Sunday on my walk I went to a small village church for the morning service. Unusually, there was no word of welcome and no coffee and chat afterwards. However, as I sat on a bench outside the church getting my things organised, an older lady who had been at the service came up to me and asked me back to her home for coffee and to meet her husband. We walked to her house, where she kindly gave me quite a substantial snack, the offer of lunch and even a shower (she was keen that I didn't misinterpret this offer!). Mary and her husband were both so kind, and very concerned for the future of the church. However, having heard about my pilgrimage, they told me about the prayer they said together each morning: thanking God for the lovely place He had put them in and asking that He help them to be good neighbours, including to strangers. I could have cried at this point. They explained how they both simply love living in the village, which they see as an oasis of peace, calm, good conduct and neighbourliness.

The Emmaus road

On several occasions when I was walking, I had the experience of people coming up from behind me and walking with me. On all these occasions I had the sense that these people were coming alongside me, supporting and encouraging me. On the first occasion, I was walking on the coastal path towards a small resort when a man came along, catching up with me and then walking with me for a few minutes. I was intrigued by the small device he had slung over his shoulder. He then told me he was a long-distance swimmer and that the device was a buoyancy aid that 'will keep me afloat if I have a heart attack in the water'. He was just off for his late-morning swim, having already done his early-morning training. He then went on ahead and at the next beach I saw him swimming directly out from the shore to a buoy at a considerable distance from the water's edge. He circled the buoy and returned to the beach. When this man had first come alongside me, I had been feeling quite tired and making very slow progress on the rather convoluted path, but chatting with him really cheered me up. I no longer felt strange and isolated; being a long-distance walker seemed rather ordinary compared to being a long-distance swimmer.

On another occasion I had to walk in quite heavy rain. There was little shelter and I was also having to walk along a road with a considerable amount of traffic. Fortunately after a while the rain stopped and I was able to take a much quieter road. I began to dry out, but still felt discouraged as there seemed to be no alternative to walking on the road and the town I was heading for seemed miles away. However, a man came alongside me on a bicycle, got off and began to chat with me. We talked for some time and he told me that he lived near the coastal path in the south-west of England and made a point of chatting to walkers he met on the path. When I told him about my dilemma of walking on the road, he showed me I had misread the map: there was an alternative route to the local town on a footpath near the coast. After a while, he parted from me on his way to his holiday accommodation.

On the third occasion, a woman appeared as if from nowhere and walked down a lane with me for some time. Before she met me that morning, I had been feeling very low, partly caused by tiredness after having been kept awake by very loud and strange noises the night before. She told me the cause of the noise would have been manoeuvres at a military base nearby. Useful and some comfort though it was to know this, just chatting with her had the effect of raising my spirits and casting away the misery that I had been feeling.

In all of these encounters I felt I was in something of an Emmaus road situation, as strangers came alongside me and kindly encouraged me. After the meeting with the man on the bike, it felt like Jesus himself might have been with me.

CHAPTER 6

'I would like to know the Lord's Prayer in Welsh.' A CROSS-CULTURAL JOURNEY

I FOUND MY experience of Welsh perhaps one of the most challenging aspects of my pilgrimage. The words 'I would like to know the Lord's Prayer in Welsh,' were spoken to me by a lady in her caravan at a campsite in north Wales. We had got talking in the washing-up room at this site and she and her husband had kindly asked me to call in and visit them in their caravan. They'd originally asked me over in the evening but as it was getting late, I declined. The next morning I felt a bit guilty about this and decided to visit them after I had packed my tent. They had described themselves as 'Christians but not very often churchgoers', so I decided to give them the booklet of prayers that I had been given whilst walking with the pilgrim group across north Wales. This contained simple but thoughtful prayers for each day of the week. It just seemed like a good idea to give it to them and, although I was using it a little, I didn't really need it and it was taking up space in my map case. They greeted me very warmly, offered me a cup of tea and seemed happy to accept the booklet of prayers. It appeared to be my giving them the prayer book that prompted her to say that she would like to know the Lord's Prayer in Welsh. Although she told me that neither of them were Welsh speakers, she said she had known the Lord's Prayer in Welsh as a child. To her it seemed to represent a faith, or even just a time, that she had lost. I apologised for my prayer booklet not being in Welsh and said I hoped she would find one, as indeed I prayed later.

And it was later that same day that I had what was probably the most significant conversation of my pilgrimage as regards the Welsh language. Anxious to ensure I was keeping to the public right of way across some farmland, I got into conversation with an elderly farmer. Having established that I was following the right route, he seemed keen to talk. I was surprised at the openness and yet the gentleness of his words. He said that it was 'a miracle' (his words) that Welsh had survived. I think it was at this point in the conversation that I apologised that we were talking in English. He remarked that he might seem slow of speech but added that sometimes two or three weeks might go by without him speaking English and so, when he did need to use the language, he felt hesitant. He also amazed me by outlining a very impressive family tree, going back centuries. It was also interesting that this man deplored the division between north and south Wales, but he said he wasn't typical in that he knew south Wales well because he bought lambs there to rear on his farm.

I had first come across bilingual church services which used both Welsh and English earlier on my walk, on the Sunday I spent in Aberdaron. Bilingual services were possible as readings done in Welsh were provided in English on the service sheet. One of the hymns was also in Welsh. However, later that day I visited the tiny church of St Maelrhys in Llanfaelrhys, in the same group of churches. I was aware that I was there about the time that a service of evening prayer would take place. Someone then arrived to take the service and asked me if I would join him.

It was obvious that there would be just the two of us. In a crass moment, I asked if we could do the service in English. As soon as I'd spoken, I realised what a thoughtless thing I'd said. The lay minister said nothing to my silly comment and we proceeded with the service in a mixture of English and Welsh. I was fairly sure that, on his own, he would have conducted and sung the service entirely in Welsh which, along with about 75% of the population of this area of Wales, was clearly his native tongue.

My next conversation as regards Welsh was fortunately rather lighter in tone. Visiting the impressive church of Llanbadarn Fawr near Aberystwyth, I got talking with a lady cleaning the church. She told me that she had studied Welsh at the University in Bangor in the 1970s (she remarked that back then, going to Bangor seemed like moving away but that it wouldn't be seen in the same way today). She told me that one of the most famous poems from medieval Wales was about this church. In his poem *Merched Llanbadarn*, the fourteenth-century poet Dafydd ap Gwilym describes coming to church at Llanbadarn Fawr to look at girls, but overhearing the girls talking about *him*.

I remarked to this lady that I didn't know any Welsh, but was slightly nonplussed when she told me that 'The word for church is *eglwys*' – one of the few words that I did actually know. Perhaps I should have been encouraged by this incident: at that point I had a Welsh vocabulary of about ten words that I could speak, perhaps twenty or thirty if I was just reading. This lady had taken my claim that I didn't know any Welsh quite literally, whereas I was indulging in a bit of false modesty. How could I then complain when she thought I didn't know a basic word such as *eglwys*?

Perhaps I should have been encouraged too by the incident a few weeks later near Llanelli when, walking into a small church, a lady there (also cleaning) said something to me in Welsh that was quite incomprehensible to me. She immediately added in English, 'Have you come far?' At least I looked like someone who could be a Welsh speaker!

Translation of the Bible into Welsh

When I was in St Asaph, I saw the Victorian monument outside the cathedral to the men responsible for the translation of the Bible into Welsh.

Having the Bible and church services in the mother tongue of the people rather than in Latin was one of the main aims of the Protestant reformers of western Europe in the sixteenth century. However, in the case of Wales, this created a problem. The English Bible was foisted on the Welsh in the reign of Edward VI when, in the Act of Uniformity of 1549, it was decreed that church services and Bible readings should be in English. This was at a time when Welsh was also banned from official use and in courts of law.

Fortunately, there was a change of heart in the reign of Elizabeth I, when in 1563 it was ordered that the Bible and the Book of Common Prayer should be translated into Welsh and used in services[31]. This led William Salesbury to work on a Welsh translation of the New Testament and parts of the prayer book. However, William Morgan, Cambridge scholar and vicar of Llanrhaeadr-ym-Mochnant in the Diocese of St Asaph, also began work on his translation of the Bible into Welsh. After various revisions, this took on a similar role to the King James Authorised Version of the Bible in English, in that it formed and shaped the language of the people, and greatly surpassed Salesbury's translation. The first edition was published in 1588 and a second edition in 1620, this remaining the leading Welsh translation until the late twentieth century.

There is also a possibility that there was a translation of part of the Bible into Welsh in the fourteenth century, although this has never been verified. Although the translation of the Bible into the vernacular, the spoken language of the people, was a demand of the Protestant reformers, in fact there had been many translations of parts of the Bible, notably the gospels and psalms, into the vernacular of the various countries of Europe in the Middle Ages. Of course, in the age before printing, these were high-status documents. It's interesting to surmise that Welsh may also have had a pre-Reformation translation.

Metrical psalms in Welsh

Arriving at a campsite in southern Snowdonia, I got into quite a long conversation with the owner and a friend of his about local things that I would find interesting and relevant to my pilgrimage. In fact, I didn't appreciate the significance of part of my conversation with these men until I got to the church in nearby Maentwrog,

The Victorian monument to William Morgan and the other men involved in the translation of the Bible into Welsh, St Asaph.

where I saw the west window commemorating Edmund Prys, who was rector there from 1572 to 1624 and 'translated the metrical psalms into Welsh'. Prys' version of the psalms was included in the 1621 Welsh edition of the Book of Common Prayer.

It's important to realise that the church at this time had nothing like the hymn or songbooks that have so characterised worship in the last two or three centuries. Singing in church before the Reformation had been in Latin, by clerics and clerical choirs. However, the Reformers were keen to follow the Biblical injunctions to worship in 'hymns, psalms and spiritual songs'. This was interpreted as allowing the use of psalms or other song-like Biblical passages in the new venture of congregational singing. Edmund Prys was by far the most successful of several Welshmen who tried to translate the psalms into songs that ordinary people, many of whom were illiterate, could memorise and sing.

For most of the psalms, he adopted an 8 7 8 7 metre (eight syllables in the first line, seven in the second, eight in the third and seven in the fourth) and an A B C B rhyming pattern in each verse. What is perhaps interesting to observe is that metrical psalms provided a stepping stone between the Gregorian chant type of singing of the medieval period and the hymn and songbooks of the modern era.

'Hedd Wyn' and St John Roberts

The small visitor centre in Trawsfynydd (in the same building as a rather splendid new hostel) has displays about two local men: 'Hedd Wyn', a local Welsh-language poet who was killed in the First World War, and St John Roberts, a Catholic martyred at Tyburn and also a local man. I found it moving that both of these men were only in their early thirties when they died, although in very different circumstances.

St John Roberts, born in the reign of Elizabeth I, was the son of one of the local gentry. He was baptised as an Anglican but converted to the Roman Catholic faith whilst travelling in Europe. After becoming a monk and then being ordained a priest, he returned to England, where it was against the law to celebrate the Roman Catholic mass. He earned respect by working amongst the poor of London for several years but was eventually arrested and executed in 1610.

Hedd Wyn, whose real name was Ellis Evans, was posthumously awarded the bardic Chair (the most prestigious prize for Welsh poetry) at the National Eisteddfod held in Birkenhead in 1917[32], having been killed at the Battle of Passchendaele a few weeks before. Each year a new Chair is made as the prize for the finest poem in the traditional Welsh form known as *cynghanedd*, but in that year the vacant chair was draped in black.

'Don't forget the areas of Wales that are now in England'

At two points in my walk I was drawn into another pilgrimage – a sub-pilgrimage, so to speak. The first was when I walked across north Wales, which was quite a major undertaking in itself, whereas the second was a short day pilgrimage from Dolgellau to nearby Cymer Abbey. This day had begun very early: I was on the road at 6 a.m., having camped only about eight miles to the north. I walked through glorious woodland and valleys on one of the most memorable mornings of my trip. I seemed to be one of the few people up and about, although soon after starting out I got a friendly wave from some cyclists who were also clearly enjoying the wonderful landscape. I headed down the valley of the River Mawddach, aiming for the village of Llanelltyd, where I knew there was an ancient church with interesting yew trees. As it was a Sunday, I was also hoping that I might attend a morning service there. I arrived at the church to see a notice in the porch giving information about a Pentecost Pilgrimage later that day from the centre of Dolgellau to the old abbey nearby. The usual Sunday service at the little church was cancelled because of this event later in the day. I was thrilled to learn about this local pilgrimage and decided to take part. I had been praying for a Sunday service to go to, and this was clearly more than I had expected. Unable to visit the church as it was locked (it was still quite early), I made my way into Dolgellau, treated myself to a good cooked breakfast and set up camp at a site on the edge of the town. I then met up with a small group of local people who were also intending to take part in this annual local pilgrimage to celebrate Pentecost.

The service itself took place in what had been the church of the ancient abbey; the first time I had ever been to a service in such a place. It was moving to think of monks over 500 years ago observing all their monastic offices in this place which has now for so long been just a ruin.

After the service there was tea and chat, and it was then that one of the clerics involved asked me about my plans for future pilgrimages and said, 'Don't forget the areas of Wales that are now in England'. I was aware that areas of Herefordshire were very Welsh in their culture, as shown particularly in place names. But his comment made me realise that some areas of the Marches, as the borderlands are known, could perhaps have ended up in modern Wales rather than in England. The comment made by this cleric gave me a greater appreciation of the arbitrary nature of the modern border.

I found myself continuing to think about what he had said, perhaps because I was beginning to realise that I would not have time on my pilgrimage to do anything but walk straight home from Llantwit Major and Cardiff, so missing out some of the area that this man had drawn my attention to. His comment also served to highlight the connections between the border area within Wales where I now live and my home county of Herefordshire.

I was already aware that the village of Weston under Penyard near my home town of Ross-on-Wye is thought to be the site of the Roman fort of Ariconium. This is one of those places, now within England, where there is some evidence for the continuation of Christianity from the Roman period into the emerging Celtic kingdoms. After the Roman withdrawal in the early fifth century, Ergyng, a small Celtic kingdom with links into what is now Monmouthshire, came into existence centred on what had been Ariconium. This is the land of Dyffrig, the Celtic saint strongly associated with Herefordshire, with four ancient churches dedicated to him in this area.

The little Celtic kingdom was gradually surrounded by Anglo Saxon territory and became subsumed into the kingdom of Mercia, although a small part, known as Archenfield, remained largely Welsh-speaking for several centuries.

Wiston Castle

An unexpected, at least to me, cultural influence on later medieval Wales was that of the Flemish. When walking towards Carmarthen, I came across Wiston Castle, which had been the stronghold of a Fleming called Wizo. The name of the castle derives from his name. Flemish people were settled in this area of west Wales by Henry I as part of his strategy for controlling Wales, the Flemings seeming originally to have fled their native land due to encroachment by sand and sea.

Diversity

As I left Swansea by walking through the rejuvenated area of the docks, I came across a new community church with a very smart-looking building. Taking a closer look, I saw that it hosted a Sunday afternoon Korean church[33]. This church perhaps reflects a little of the ethnic and cultural diversity of much of modern Wales.

There are considerable Christian links between Wales and Korea, notably because the son of a south Wales minister was martyred in Korea in the mid-nineteenth century after his missionary endeavours went seriously wrong. In spite of this, Robert Jermain Thomas is seen in Korea as having brought the Christian faith to the country.

Today, Christianity is strong in South Korea, with perhaps a third of the population being Christians. Each year, many Koreans visit Hanover Chapel near Abergavenny *(Y Fenni)* where Thomas' father was the minister.

Another aspect of ethnic and cultural diversity that I came across was that of migrants coming from the European Union, such as a young lady from Poland whom I met at a campsite in west Wales. We had a long chat, discussing our different understanding of culture in Wales, England and Poland. She was staying at the campsite whilst she did an upholstery course.

CHAPTER 7

'Are you a traveller?'
THINGS RELATING TO
CHILDREN AND LEARNING

ONE INTERESTING FEATURE I saw in churches several times early on my pilgrimage was an Easter garden. These varied from the very simple to larger and more complex creations. These 'gardens' are a way of representing the story of the empty tomb on Easter morning when some of the women amongst Jesus' disciples went to the place where Jesus' body had been placed late the previous afternoon, only to find his body missing. They would have been going to the tomb early on the Sunday morning to prepare the body properly for its final burial.

All you need to make an Easter garden is some sort of container, a few stones to represent the empty sepulchre (in Jesus' time this would have been more like a small cave), a few twigs or something similar to fashion the cross, and some greenery or flowers. The photo shows a simple but rather charming Easter garden seen in a church in the Black Mountains in mid Wales.

Easter gardens, which might be made by children or adults, are part of a long line of artefacts and traditions that try to present Bible stories in a visual form. Even with today's almost universal literacy, using different media for stories and – in the case of Easter gardens – giving people not just something to see but something to make too, should encourage more active learning and a greater engagement with the Christian faith.

A simple Easter garden in a church in mid Wales.

Children in church

One thing I was keen to find out about as I walked was the provision made for children in the different churches that I visited. My first interesting discovery, and something that I had never seen before, was of a children's altar in a church in mid Wales, something I saw again a week or so later. It was unclear at either of these places whether the altar was a 'real' one: that is, whether the Eucharist was celebrated at them. I presumed that this was not the case and that such 'altars' were for what could be described as religious play. To my even greater surprise, near Ruthin in Flintshire I visited a church where a small 'play' church had been built at the back of the nave. This delightful and colourful wooden structure contained little chairs for the 'congregation', miniature vestments to wear and, again, a tiny altar.

I continued to be surprised by how much thought, time and effort had been put into providing facilities for children, even in small country churches. I would go so far as to say it was almost the norm for churches to have a child-orientated area. Whether these were for the use of parents and young children during services to help keep children amused or were for weekday use by parent and toddler groups was usually unclear, but I imagined it was often for both. I also saw careful provision of what looked like craft tables in churches for the use of older children, perhaps where it wasn't practical to offer a Sunday school or similar group every week. One development of this idea which really impressed me was providing simple activities for children visiting the church, which I saw at Llanina near New Quay in Ceredigion. Here the tiny church near the seashore was especially geared towards tourists, including children, who were provided with simple colouring activities to do and then take away as a reminder of their visit. This would give them something meaningful to do whilst adults with them looked around the church.

I was also surprised by how many churches were offering 'Messy Church' or similar informal services aimed at families and children. To those unfamiliar with the Messy Church concept, this is a simple form of worship which involves craft activities (hence 'messy') followed by a child-friendly short service and then a shared meal. I even read, in a diocesan magazine, about 'Messy Cathedral' which, again, was new to me.

However, it was at a small church near Carmarthen that I was privileged to join in with a Sunday morning service where children were integrated into the life of the church in a simple yet rather lovely way; I'm not sure I have ever seen a congregation more fully represent the family of the church in such a simple and yet challenging way. At this church, several children happily coloured and read in the choir stalls, in full view of the congregation and behind the clergyman, who led the service from the top of the nave. One delightful moment was as he was just a minute or so into his sermon, when one of the children jumped up and quickly showed the vicar his colouring. This was very briefly admired before the child happily returned to the choir stalls. This was the only interruption until the moment came for the bread and wine to be brought to the priest for communion. Without any prompting and at exactly the right moment, the children brought the gifts to the altar and then, without any fuss, returned to the choir stalls and resumed their colouring. Particularly moving at this church was the way that the whole congregation took communion together, standing 'in the round', the children also joining the circle and receiving a blessing.

Easter tableau in a church in north Wales.

'Lo, children are an heritage and gift that cometh of the Lord'
Matthew 18 tells us that we, as adults, have to become like children to enter the kingdom of heaven. Jesus' rebuke, 'Except ye be converted, and become as little children, ye shall not enter into the kingdom of heaven,' was addressed to the disciples as they squabbled over who was the greatest. A child then becomes a symbol of the humility and lowliness we need in order to experience God's kingdom.

In our culture, we often look at children and childhood in a different way to how they would have been perceived in the first century. Our culture rightly gives the welfare and well-being of children a very high priority. But Jesus taking the image of a child to show what he wanted to teach can still speak to us today. We expect children to learn from us, but here we see that we can and must learn from them. I find it quite challenging to think about what I can learn from children: perhaps their trust, joy and optimism.

Church schools in Wales

I was surprised to see so many Church in Wales schools on my pilgrimage, such as that at Llanbedr near where I live, which I passed on the first day of my walk. I had imagined that because the Church in Wales is disestablished from the state, church schools would not be as obvious as they are in rural areas of England. However, in many villages and towns I passed through, the primary school was a church school.

In Wales there are about 170 church schools, although this number includes primary and secondary schools. This may seem a lot, but in England there are about 5,000 church schools, both primary and secondary. It would seem from this that although there may seem to be a surprising number of church schools in Wales, the proportion of children educated in such schools is proportionately higher in England. This presumably reflects the strength of non-conformity in Wales.

The Travelling Schools

The very extensive graveyard at Llandre (*Llanfihangel Genau'r Glyn*), north of Aberystwyth, includes the grave of Edward Lewis, who died in 1843. The information board near his grave tells us that he was a teacher for 35 years in the Circulating Welsh Charity Schools founded by Griffith Jones, the Rector of Llanddowror (*Maes-y-lan*) in Carmarthenshire. It is not known precisely when this chain of schools was founded, but by 1737 there were 40 of them. These Circulating Schools provided education in the less busy winter months, using itinerant teachers like Edward Lewis. Adults as well as children attended, in a time when there was no state provision of education.

A few weeks later I walked through Llanddowror, although the church there was unfortunately closed. However, the next day I walked past the church at Merthyr, a few miles away on the way to Carmarthen. This church was where Bridget Bevan, the wealthy philanthropist who funded the Circulating Schools, worshipped. She was born into the local Vaughan family at nearby Derllys and was baptised and married in the church. Although I had initially just passed by near this church, by chance I met a former churchwarden, who took me down to it, allowing me to see inside and sharing with me a little of the remarkable story of Bridget Bevan.

The Knitted Bible

Walking into a town in mid Wales, I saw signs for 'The Knitted Bible'. I had heard of this but knew very little about it, so I decided to go and look at the exhibition in the local Baptist church. There I spent a good hour looking at the 30 or so miniature scenes depicting events from a wide variety of Biblical stories, such as Joseph and his brothers, Zacchaeus up a tree trying to see Jesus, and the wedding at Cana. The figures were all about ten inches tall and they, and most of the 'props', were all carefully and rather delightfully knitted. The Baptist Church which was hosting the exhibition had been able to welcome an encouraging number of visitors, including several school groups. Each scene included the relevant Bible story to read, for those who weren't familiar with what was being portrayed.

We might like to think about the place of the Bible and its teaching not just in our own lives but in our life together as churches, and the role of the Bible in our nation both in the past and now in the present. In my own life, when I take time to read and study the Bible, I am always amazed by how wonderful and exciting it is to read.

But it is not necessarily an easy read, and lovely though it is to see it in a charming, knitted form, the Bible often does not give us easy answers to many of the issues that we face either in our own lives or as a wider society today. However, this should be an encouragement to listen to, read and study the Bible in a balanced, fresh and informed way, remembering also those areas of the world where owning a Bible is rare or even illegal.

The Knitted Bible in Newtown, mid Wales. The scene depicted is the story of the wedding at Cana in Galilee.

'Are you a traveller?'

I was asked this by some children at a rather urban site near Swansea (*Abertawe*). The children were, of course, using the word 'traveller' in the modern sense, where previous generations would have said 'gypsy'. I really enjoyed my conversation with these delightful girls of about 6 and 8 and the two boys hovering around nearby. The children asked all sorts of basic questions about where I got food and so on, but it was this question that really struck me because, in my mind at least, it called into question my status in society. In their young eyes I was possibly someone from a social group often seen as very different from ordinary 'settled' people. I was perhaps fortunate in dealing with this question because, as a teacher, I had worked in a school with a considerable number of students from traveller families, the vast majority of whom were delightful to teach and very well behaved. Of course, in answering the children's question, I did not know what their experience of travellers was, or indeed if they just knew of travellers by repute. I replied that I was not a traveller – taking care, I hope, not to disparage travellers in any way – that I had a house to live in and that I was living in my tent just for a while and by choice. I told them I was walking around Wales, later regretting that I didn't talk about my walk more specifically as a pilgrimage and wondering if I had patronised or underestimated these children. But the thought that they had considered whether I might be a traveller (and it was a thoughtfully-asked question) stayed with me, perhaps because of its implications for my status in the community.

This issue of status had occurred to me various times over the walk. If I was walking down a road with considerable traffic and perhaps outside an area associated with walking and outdoor pursuits, I was aware that I might appear to be a vagrant of some sort. One lady campsite owner even said jokingly to me, 'Be careful you don't look like a bag lady.' I don't think I actually did look like a bag lady: my pack was nice and neat and my clothes deliberately chosen to suit me and my occupation as a long-distance walker; not for me tin mugs dangling from my pack and so on. I had reasonably smart and well-fitting black walking trousers and a 'pilgrim' jumper in a distinctive and very practical style. I even had my hair cut and tinted at a hairdressers along the route so as to avoid my grey roots showing. Indeed, it was reassuring when someone remarked to me, 'You look very well turned out for someone who's been on the road for two months.'

But the issue of status remained in a society where speed, ease of movement and affluence are so greatly prized. Perhaps related to this was the inference by a few people that I was backpacking because I couldn't afford to do anything else. Once or twice I felt pained by this suggestion, particularly when it came from an affluent Christian I met who seemed unable to grasp that walking was part of my pilgrimage: it was what I felt God wanted me to do and was done by choice. Perhaps I just had to let go of that one.

CHAPTER 8

'It's the continuity of these sites that amazes me' OBSERVING EARLY CHURCH HISTORY IN THE LANDSCAPE

ON MY PILGRIMAGE I found that I learned about lots of new things, often encouraged by the enthusiasm and knowledge of others. One area that I was drawn into was that of the great ancient yew trees of Wales.

On one of my days off with my husband early in the trip, we had visited the huge dams of the Elan Valley and in the bookshop there I bought a book about the yew trees of Wales. I then left this in our van as I walked on the next day as I didn't feel I could justify carrying the extra weight. However, just flicking through a few pages, I could see that yew trees were a source of great interest.[34]

A few days later I was camping at a tiny site near another great reservoir at Lake Vyrnwy. A young couple were the only other people at the site and, in the evening, they beckoned me over to share their campfire for a while. The young man of thirty or so told me that he was a tree surgeon; he had been brought up in that area as a child but had moved away. He wanted to show his girlfriend something of the local area that was still so important to him. They asked me about what I was doing. Having outlined my progress so far and my plans, he remarked, 'It's the continuity of these sites that amazes me, but what really interests me…' – and at this point the young lady interjected with, 'You're not going to believe this!' – before he then completed his sentence with, 'what really interests me is the yew trees.' I was then able to tell him about the book I had bought and share a little about the yew tree sites I had already seen on my walk. As a tree surgeon, he was able to offer more specialised knowledge and interest.

From then on I made more of an effort to research possible yew tree sites I could visit and to read the book on my days off. All I had known about these trees before I set off was that they are common in churchyards and that sometimes they are planted in a ring, as indeed they are in my home church at Llanelly (*Llanelli*, but not to be confused with the more well-known one in Carmarthenshire), near Gilwern. However, the book was a fascinating read and certainly encouraged me to give these trees a higher profile on my walk.

I had not realised that the churchyards of Wales are a very significant habitat for yew trees in Europe, and a very high proportion of ancient yew trees (defined as yews with a girth of more than 800 cm) are in Welsh churchyards. The book also briefly dealt with whether yew trees were especially significant in Celtic culture and whether they were held to be symbolic by the early Christians in Wales. As a historian, I was pleased to find that no extravagant claims unjustified by evidence were being made for the yew trees. However, the considerable number of trees that can reasonably be dated to the early medieval period does strongly suggest that these trees were seen as symbolic of some Christian beliefs, and so important to plant near sacred sites.

What especially fascinated me was that a few of these trees can be dated to the very early Christian period, the so-called Age of the Saints. The magnificent yew tree at Llanerfyl was one such example that I was able to see. This tree, as with several others in Wales, is used to provide evidence to build up a picture, so to speak, of a site as belonging to these very early years in the sixth century, or even before that in the later Romano-British period.

Yew trees in Welsh churchyards

Learning about yew trees and observing some magnificent specimens became an unexpected delight whilst on my pilgrimage. The yew *Taxus baccata* is native to the British Isles and notable examples are also found in churchyards in Scotland and England (although ancient specimens no longer exist in Ireland), but a greatly disproportionate number of yew trees are found in Welsh churchyards. Considerable and sometimes conflicting claims have also been made for the age of some of these trees: in some cases supposedly three thousand years or so. This has been combined, in some quarters, with a view of the trees as possessing a mythical or spiritual property. There are also questions as to whether these trees had any practical purpose. All of these factors have combined to create a fascinating area for study. However, all of this is dwarfed, literally, by the wonderful presence of these trees in so many churchyards. I would go so far as to say that yew trees were one of the highlights of my walk.

I saw many specimens on my pilgrimage, including some of the most ancient in Wales. Especially notable was the tree at Llanerfyl, where the collapsed crown dominates the churchyard, but also at Bettws Newydd with its tree of over 10 m in girth and large internal stem, a feature of yew tree growth patterns. These are well-known examples, but lesser-known trees are also lovely to see, such as at Llanfaredd near Builth Wells, where a tree of over 9 m in girth is to be found in the tiny churchyard tucked away behind a farm.

But how realistic are the claims made for these trees as regards their age, their alleged spiritual properties and possible practical uses? Concerning the age of yew trees, it has been pointed out that the only ones we can reliably date are those relatively young trees for which we have a planting date. For others a variety of factors have to be considered, although the girth of the tree is usually the most significant characteristic. However, the patterns of growth among older yews mean that girth is often difficult or even impossible to measure because the trunk of an ancient yew is often very uneven and split, to say nothing of sections rotting away or breaking off. Even if the girth can be measured, other things have to be taken into account, such as the amount of hollowing and decay (the most ancient bit of the tree may not even exist any more), and the history of the site itself. As regards the most ancient trees seen in churchyards such as Llanerfyl, it is reasonable to think that the yews are old enough to have been planted when the site was first Christianised and that these trees do go back to the age of the early saints. Those trees that are ancient but perhaps not quite as old, such as at Llanfaredd, could indicate that the site belongs more to the tenth or eleventh centuries, that the existing tree was a replacement or that for some reason yew trees were not planted in the earliest days of Christian use of the site.

It is also often thought that the early Christians in Wales inherited a belief in the mystical or spiritual properties of yew trees from pagan times. This too is difficult to verify as, although trees in general seem to have been revered by the Celts, there is not much evidence that yews in particular were seen as special. The limited evidence to the contrary comes from archaeological finds such as the tankard made of yew found near Newport in south Wales and dated to about two thousand years ago. This large item seems to have been used for communal or ceremonial drinking. Yew wood also seems to have been used in some Christian artefacts in the early Celtic church, notably the Kells crozier from Ireland, of which the wooden core is yew. This bishop's staff dates back to between the ninth and eleventh centuries.

However, we are faced with the fact that a large proportion of Welsh churchyards have ancient yews, and if we take those churches and churchyards that have other ancient features, the proportion of associated ancient yew trees gets even greater. Thus, it's reasonable to assume that yews did have a special significance for the early Christians in Wales, even if we don't know on exactly what basis. One possibility as regards their significance is that the yew, as an evergreen, could have been seen as a sign of the eternal life Christians believe we will enjoy with God, or as a sign of God's faithful benevolence. If the pagan Celts did revere the yew, perhaps also based on its evergreen nature, it would not seem unreasonable for these ideas to have been developed in the Christian era.

There is also evidence that from the eighth century evergreen foliage was used to represent palm branches in the observance of Palm Sunday. In northern Europe one obvious substitute for palm was the yew. The custom also developed of burning the 'palms' to provide ash for Ash Wednesday the following year. It is possible that yew trees in churchyards were a source of suitable foliage for these liturgical uses.

There may also have been practical issues that encouraged the placing of yews in early church sites. It is commonly known that yews are dangerous, sometimes fatal, to livestock (only the berries are not poisonous) and so it would seem to make sense to plant them in an area that even in the earliest days may have been enclosed, perhaps by a bank and simple palisade. This would clearly have been a disincentive to allowing animals to graze in the enclosure and, it could be presumed, would have added to the sense of sanctity.

There is also the possibility that in a landscape generally more wooded than today, yew trees may have acted as a marker, as most surrounding trees would have been deciduous with lighter-coloured foliage. Yews may have guided people to the church site.

Another practical use for yew trees that is often mentioned is that they were used as a source of wood for longbows. However, this should be discounted as the growth patterns of *Taxus baccata* in northern Europe make the wood unsuitable for longbows, and the wood needed for them was imported from southern Europe.

Holy wells and inscribed stones

The young tree surgeon I spoke to was fascinated by the continuity at church sites in Wales; that is, not just the great length of time that worship or veneration of a deity has gone on at a particular place, but also the continuity with different belief systems at the same site.

The revering of yew trees is seen as possibly providing continuity with previous pagan culture, and the same is often suggested of holy wells, of which there are many in Wales. As with yew trees, it is often asserted that springs of water had particular significance in pre-Christian pagan times. This is related to the issue of how far Christianity was built on pre-existing culture: that is, the degree of continuity with pagan Celtic practices and beliefs.

Springs clearly had great practical use as a reliable source

The ancient yew tree at Llanerfyl. Note that what may appear to be separate tree trunks is, in fact, all the same tree. The central section of the tree has hollowed away completely, a feature of very old yew trees.

of water, on which early settlements depended. Early churches in Wales would have had that same practical need for water. The early Christians in Wales would also have needed water for baptism and for the washing of communion vessels.

But the close proximity of many early church sites in Wales to springs of water is believed by many to reflect the reverence for water in the earlier pagan culture. The inference is that some of the early churches were built on sites that were already important in a spiritual sense and that the missionary activity of the early saints was made more straightforward by adopting existing sites, thus giving converts some familiarity and avoiding what was seen as unnecessary conflict.[35] Also, potential 'rival' pagan worship would be limited or even prevented by the taking over of those sites by Christians.

We know little about how and why water, and especially springs of water, were revered in Celtic religion, but there does seem to have been an association with springs as places of healing and this seems to be reinforced by the well-documented and frequent use of springs for this purpose once Wales had been Christianised.

On my walk I saw evidence in many forms of the holy wells that have been built over springs of water to provide better access down to the water source and also to dignify the surroundings. Holywell in Flintshire is clearly the example par excellence of a holy well. The size and beauty of the well chapel at Holywell sets it apart from other holy wells we see today. In pre-Reformation Wales, chapels built over sources of rivers would have been more widespread, although I think we can safely assume Holywell would always have been the grandest.

More typical would have been Llangelynnin above the Conwy Valley, where the holy well is inside the churchyard surrounded by a modest enclosure and steps to get down to the level of the water. Sites such as Llangelynnin make us think and speculate about how such places could have originated as places of Christian worship. Perhaps an early saint adopted the site with its convenient water supply, acting almost as a guardian of the site. A simple chapel was built, and a basic hut for the saint to live in. Such a scenario leaves open the question as to whether the water was already perceived as having healing properties or whether it acquired such a reputation through association with the saint. There is nothing at Llangelynnin to show current activity relating to the well as a place of healing.

But this is not the case at Patricio, a well not far from my home in the Black Mountains and somewhere I visited on the first day of my pilgrimage. This is a glorious place on a hillside above a very quiet valley. The site is believed to go back to the sixth century and to have originated as the hermitage of Saint Issui. The well is a short distance from the churchyard and when I visited was festooned with all sorts of small items left by visitors, making something of a small shrine. When I visited, the well was dry, but it still flows when there has been heavy rain. The large quantity of small items – ribbons, beads, pebbles and so on – is a sign of the considerable activity here, as people had left tokens of various types[36].

The reasons why people leave such things at holy wells is

perhaps just as open to question now as it was a thousand or more years ago. Francis Jones devotes a fascinating few pages to this issue in his book The Holy Wells of Wales. His analysis can perhaps be summarised as suggesting that people left clothes behind as a token of the healing they believed they had received. The clothes then deteriorated into rags. This led to the custom of tying small bits of fabric or ribbons onto trees or bushes surrounding the well.

There is also the ancient practice of dropping or throwing items into water courses or wells. There are many examples of archaeological finds, often of weapons or coins, where significant items appear to have been deliberately left. The items themselves seem to have had a symbolic meaning, as well as the method of depositing them. This may all seem a long way from the clutter of objects at Patricio, but the leaving of objects significant to the visitor may well represent a continuity with the distant and even pre-Christian past that those who leave such things may well be quite unaware of.[37]

Other holy wells I visited included Ffynnon Beuno in Clynnog Fawr on the Llŷn Peninsula, one of several wells named after St Beuno in north Wales[38]. The well housing here is a large and well-maintained structure on a frequently-used road on the edge of the village. When I visited, there was plenty of water but no sign of any expectations of divine intervention; all in all it appeared rather sanitised. This is an example of a well that it's reasonable to speculate was actually blessed or used by the saint whose name it takes: Beuno is a well-known saint closely associated with Clynnog Fawr.

Another well I visited was St David's Well (indicated in English on the Ordnance Survey map) just north of Porthcawl on the south Wales coast. This is one of over 30 wells in Wales dedicated to St David, and it's not known if this one was associated with St David in anything but name[39]. Although a small information board nearby gives some information, there's no indication of any contemporary veneration of the well taking place either. There is a very large, rough slab covering the well. Although the steps are still just visible behind a small locked gate, there is, unfortunately, considerable undergrowth and some litter.

Other evidence for continuity at Christian sites in Wales comes in the form of inscribed stones. Although inscribing on a stone and then setting it in a particular place may well be a development of the frequent standing stones of the Bronze Age, the inscribed stones of early Christian Wales are interesting because they appear to provide evidence for continuity with Britain as it was under Roman rule, or certainly in the century or so afterwards. They might even, very tentatively, be continuous with Christianity as it was in the later Roman period.

Some of these very early inscribed stones are reliably dated by experts to the later Roman period in Wales or to the Romano-British period in the hundred years or so after the end of Roman rule. The evidence for this is the style of the Latin and the style of the lettering itself. That they are specifically Christian memorials can only be pieced together from the site in which they are found or are known to have been in, the lack of specific pagan language or symbols, the similarity to memorials in other places that can be definitely identified as Christian and language that strongly suggests a Christian origin.

One example is the ancient stone in the church (it was in the churchyard until the nineteenth century) at Llanerfyl, which dates to the later Romano-British period. The Llanerfyl stone refers to a girl of thirteen years of age whose name is difficult to decipher. However, the name of her father is given, and this may be a Latinised form of the name of a local chieftain.

Other stones that I saw which are especially interesting as regards continuity with Romano-British culture are the well-known ones in the church at Aberdaron. This pair of stones, found at a farm on the headland above Aberdaron, have Latin inscriptions which strongly suggest a Christian community, perhaps the predecessor of the church site in Aberdaron, or associated with the island of Bardsey nearby[40]. Another notable stone in the same area is the Llangian Stone near Abersoch. The Llangian Stone is unique in being the only memorial of its age in Britain which refers to the profession of the deceased; in this case Melus, who is described as a doctor.

Whereas the stones at Llanerfyl, Aberdaron and Llangian point to late Romano-British culture in Wales, some other ancient inscribed stones have evidence of ogham script on them, providing evidence for the close links between some areas of Wales and Ireland at this time.

Just how these countries influenced each other and which direction the traffic was going in can be difficult to unravel. One fundamental difference between them is that Ireland was never part of the Roman Empire, whereas Wales was. One theory is that the Christian faith first reached Ireland from Wales during the Roman period.

Ogham was an early alphabet in use in Ireland from the fourth to sixth centuries, being used to write down early Irish. However, ogham stones in Wales, of which there are 35 undisputed examples, nearly always include the same or very similar words, written in Latin. This is clearly a fascinating juxtaposition of languages for all sorts of reasons, notably the pervading influence of Roman culture and language even outside the areas formally under Roman rule.

What is also interesting about these stones with ogham inscriptions (which look rather like a modern barcode and are written on the edge of the stone) is that they are in two main clusters in Wales. These are south-west Wales and the Brecon area and, as such, are key evidence for the interaction between Wales and Ireland in this period and also for Irish settlement in Wales. On my pilgrimage I saw three stones with ogham inscriptions in churches in west Wales, these being the one in St Thomas' Church, St Dogmaels (which was found in the grounds of the abbey alongside the church), and the two stones found in the church in Nevern in north Pembrokeshire.

Evidence for early Irish settlement in Wales is also found in the number of churches dedicated to the Irish saint, Brigid. I visited one in Llansantffraed, south of Aberaeron on the Ceredigion coast, a church with a very striking pre-Norman font with lovely Celtic-style patterns. What is interesting about place names derived from St Brigid is that when they have come into Welsh, the word *sant* (saint) has been included, which never happened when Welsh saints' names were used in place names.

Welsh-Breton saints

When I was camping near Corwen in Denbighshire in north Wales, I got into conversation with a Belgian couple in a camper van. They told me that they were part way through a tour of the UK and Ireland, starting in south Wales, crossing then by ferry to Ireland, driving up through the Irish Republic and into Northern Ireland, going on the ferry to Stranraer in southern Scotland, down through the Pennines and the north-west of England and then into north Wales, where I met them. Their next stop was to be Snowdonia. I was beyond impressed with this couple's itinerary, and especially that their tour had taken in so much of the Celtic seaboard of the western side of the British Isles. I asked them if they had noticed cultural similarities on their travels, which they said they had. As French speakers, they were also intrigued that the local church at Corwen was reputedly founded by two monks from Brittany, Mael and Sulien. These two men seem to have been part of a group of missionaries from Brittany who included the more well-known St Cadfan. This group also seems to have included the saints Trillo and Twrog. I was able to visit churches thought to be founded by the last two, at nearby Llandrillo and Maentwrog near Porthmadog.

What is perhaps surprising and challenging is the international nature of the early medieval church. The end of the Roman Empire in western Europe in the early fifth century led to considerable unrest, including migration from Wales, Cornwall and Devon to what we know as Brittany. This created links between these areas that were useful to the Christian missionaries as they sought areas in which to settle as hermits and to minister to local people. These links were reinforced by similar Brittonic languages – the precursors of Welsh, Breton and Cornish – and family ties, especially amongst the elite groups of the time (it is noticeable how many of the early saints are described as the sons and daughters of kings). With some of these early saints, it is difficult to unravel which 'nationality' (itself a concept that does not belong to this age) they were. It's probably easiest to try to see them as they saw themselves, as led by God.

Roman remains

One day, walking through the southern edges of Snowdonia, I visited the remains of a Roman fort and amphitheatre north of the village of Trawsfynydd. This is in a landscape rich in Roman remains.

The Roman fort at Tomen y Mur has had a few walls rebuilt to give an idea of how it would once have looked. To arrive at the fort, you take a minor road to the west off the A470, and there's then a track to the site. There are also the very incomplete remains of a small amphitheatre near the car park.

This area was served by the Roman road long known as Sarn Helen. The course of the road is classified by Ordnance Survey as an 'other route with public access' from the Roman Kilns above the Trawsfynydd Holiday Village. This is an easy but good track (I met a couple up there exploring in their Land Rover, meeting up with them three times!) with fabulous views of the Rhinog Mountains.

Christianity is believed to have arrived in Wales (as in England) during the Roman occupation, probably by the third century AD. However, it seems to have been more associated with urbanised areas around Roman settlements. Although it is thought that there was continuity between the Christianity of Roman Britain and the Christian faith in Wales after the Romans left at the end of the fourth century, it is difficult to find conclusive evidence for this.

The area around Llantwit Major can be used as an example of the difficulty in establishing this continuity. This was a heavily Romanised area with two notable villas that have been excavated and also a major Roman road. Near the villa at Caermead, just to the north of the modern town, several burials from the late Roman period which may well be Christian have been found. Also, a few miles away, at the villa in Llandough (*Llandochau Fach*) near Penarth, there was found to be an extensive late Roman cemetery. This cemetery appears to have been in continuous use into the early medieval period, where the site continued to develop into an early church.

It would be reasonable to speculate that there could be a link between these possible early Christian burials and the notable church and centre of learning at Llantwit Major known to have been founded by St Illtud in around 500 AD. Nevertheless, however logical links between the villas and this early church – and therefore between the Roman period and the Age of the Saints – might seem, no such links have ever been established.

Llanerfyl

Llanerfyl is a place that it's easy to drive through. It's on the relatively fast A458 on the way to Dolgellau, and I have certainly driven through it several times. To someone who's interested in ancient churches, what appears to be a rather drab Victorian rebuild doesn't give much incentive to stop.

However, the small parish church of St Erfyl contains several very interesting features. Near the altar are the remains of a medieval shrine which would have contained an image of St Erfyl and would have been processed around the church. There is also an earlier reliquary – a little like a miniature church – which would have contained relics, supposedly of the saint. These artefacts are reminders of the cult of saints which was very much a feature of late medieval Wales.

There is also the ancient stone discussed earlier. Near the door to the church is a very scholarly exposition about these interesting features, written in the mid-twentieth century. Apart from this, there wasn't any information for visitors when I visited, which is a great pity[41]. Outside there's a roughly circular churchyard with the very ancient yew tree and a well – although the latter is difficult to find – not far away.

What adds to the interest of this site is that several Roman roads passed nearby and it may have been on something of an interchange. This leads to speculation that the site as a place of Christian worship may have originated in the late Roman or immediate post-Roman period.

Llannau

It is, of course, quite impossible to travel around Wales and not be struck by the very large number of place names made up of *Llan* with an additional element, which is often a personal name, or derived from a name. Although there are many exceptions, such as *Llan* combined with a geographical feature, in many cases the additional element is the name of a saint, well-known or obscure. Place names of this type are believed to date from as early as the late seventh century; this practice of naming continuing until the tenth century, by which time most of these distinctive place names were established. The word itself is related to the English word 'lawn' and came to be used for land (also a related word) set aside for religious use. *Llannau* (the plural form) have also been described using terms such as 'holy enclosure' and 'sacred space', both interesting expressions.

Leaving aside the issues of how *llannau* contributed to the development of place names and parishes as units of church administration, how they were formed in the landscape and what remains of them today are perhaps two of the most interesting aspects of older church sites in Wales.

One characteristic that is seen as typical of *llannau* is that they are often roughly circular or ovoid. If we were marking out an area we would, in the modern world, usually think of giving it straight sides. However, early *llannau* probably indicate places where the enclosure was the first notable demarcation in the landscape, so there was no need to fit in with existing boundaries, except in some cases where these were geographical features, e.g. a stream.

It is also sometimes suggested that the curved or circular shape was based on rounded demarcations being seen as more 'spiritual' in the culture of the time, itself a relic of earlier pre-Christian features such as stone circles.

I was also intrigued to see, when walking across north Wales, the circular enclosure of a contemporary community, which perhaps shows us a little of how the landscape may have looked a thousand years ago or more. This modern enclosure is not religious in any way (it is there for agricultural and market-gardening purposes), but it echoes a more ancient landscape where more rounded shapes would have been more obvious than they are today.

In addition, *llanau* do not usually seem to have been founded in anything we could call a village, but in places some distance from settlements. As many may have originated as hermitages, this is perhaps not surprising. Although in many cases a village or hamlet has now grown up around them, they are part of a landscape of isolated farms and small communities; this, at least in part, explains why many village churches in Wales are some distance from the modern settlement.

Another notable feature of *llanau* is their great variation in size. Some, such as Llancarfan in Glamorgan, are very large. It is thought that these may have been sites that grew to become *clasau*, these being rather like seminaries that provided clergy for a wider area.[42] At the opposite end of the scale, some, such as Llanfaredd, are very small.

Related to this is the issue of how far the modern churchyard equates with the much earlier enclosure of the *llan*. Some churchyards contain raised banks, which seem to indicate the boundary, or part of it, of an older but smaller *llan* – Nantmel in Powys is an example of this. In some cases there are also indications of a *llan* beyond the existing churchyard and sometimes of a double enclosure, as at Llangian near Abersoch. The survival of banks marking the *llan* also draws attention to the means by which the *llan* was enclosed. It would seem likely that these banks were topped with a wattle (*bangorwaith*) fence – which is a possible root of the place name Bangor.

It would seem that *llanau* became sacred spaces through the presence there of a saint, at least in the informal sense of someone whose devotion to God and sanctity of life set them apart. It would seem that saints were then buried in their *llan*, perhaps followed by other Christian burials. The presumably simple hut and wooden cross of the very early *llan* eventually led to a separate though still simple church and perhaps additional huts for followers or later disciples.

'These churches show their prayer walks'

This comment was made over coffee after church on the Llŷn Peninsula. Having been asked by a vicar on holiday why I was making a pilgrimage around Wales, I mentioned two factors: that it was a prayer walk, and that I was especially interested in the age of the saints. He made the very interesting observation that the dedication of many churches to the same Welsh saints was an indicator of the prayer walks they had undertaken. He said a 'room' would have been kept for them in each place, in a similar way to the stories of Elijah and Elisha in the Old Testament.

This was all quite a revelation to me at the time. I was aware that saints' dedications were often clustered in particular areas, but this comment fascinated me. It was made all the more interesting in that these 'clusters' could have originated from the walks of those early saints, given that now I was walking too.

However, even at the time of this conversation, it did all sound perhaps a little romantic, and an element of the early history of the church in Wales for which we have no direct evidence. It was a view encouraged by the historian E G Bowen in his books about the Celtic saints. Bowen, originally a geographer, was born in Carmarthen in 1900.[43]

That there are clusters of dedications to particular saints is certainly the case, but to see the sites in these clusters as results of the saint's founding of churches as he visited that area is certainly an oversimplification.

Hermits

I came across stories of hermits in several places on my pilgrimage. Not far from my home, the church of St Issui in Patricio is believed to have originated as his hermitage on the steep valley side, close to the well named after him. The church is unusual in having an additional shrine chapel attached to the west end of the building. This is supposed to be the site of Issui's cell and of his burial. Today it is a quiet place set apart for prayer and reflection, with a striking modern sculpture of the sixth-century saint.

Pursuing the life of a hermit was a choice in early medieval religious life that followed the acceptance of Christianity and its legality within the Roman Empire. Once the Roman persecutions had ended and increasing areas of Europe became Christianised, there was a trend towards a substitute suffering through seeking the isolation of a hermitage.

It's likely that many early church sites in Wales started out as hermitages. However, the hermits, in life or in death, often seem to have attracted followers. It would also seem that as small monasteries developed, individual monks would sometimes be allowed to settle in a hermitage at some distance from the monastery.

St Cyngar

I spent several days walking up the south side of the Llŷn Peninsula, which (as I've mentioned) I know something of from childhood holidays. Whilst walking towards Porthmadog through the lovely seaside village of Borth-y-gest, I called in at the local church, dedicated to St Cyngar. It was explained that Cyngar had spent some time as a hermit on a small island near Criccieth (*Cricieth*). This really appealed to me. The coast around this area can seem rather tame now, but I liked the idea of an early saint marooning himself on an island there for the sake of drawing closer to God.

Clas churches

We know very little about how the early church in Wales was actually organised, but what does seem to be reasonably clear is that some churches became larger, evolving into monasteries which included monks and priests who may have acted as clergy to the surrounding area and also as founders of churches further afield. These 'sending' or 'mother' churches are sometimes referred to as *clas* churches – *clasau* in the plural. Their larger size and greater influence may have arisen because of larger endowments or gifts from wealthy lay people, or because of the energy of individuals associated with them.

One such example is Llanbadarn Fawr, now on the edge of Aberystwyth but in the early medieval period the main church of the area.

When I visited, I was impressed with the magnificent Norman church that exists there now: the remnant of the Benedictine[44] priory on the site. However, the small museum of ancient inscribed stones inside the church hints at the much earlier *clas* church on this site, founded by St Padarn in the sixth century. St Padarn is described as both an abbot and a bishop, roles which were then quite fluid.

My walk also included other *clas* sites such as Llancarfan, founded by St Cadoc (*Cattwg* in Welsh) in the sixth century, and Glasbury, not far from my home. Here the *clas* status of the early church is preserved in the Welsh name of the village *Y Glas ar Wy*, 'the monastic community on the Wye'.

Disserth, the desert

The earliest form of Christian monasticism was amongst the desert monks of Egypt from the late third century onwards. They sought closeness to God in a literal desert. Although the exact links between monks in the Egyptian desert and the early Welsh church are unclear, the idea of seeking God in a desert seems to have been something the early saints in Wales were aware of. Disserth near Llandrindod in Powys may derive its name from originally being someone's desert, from the Latin *desertum*, corrupted over time into Disserth.

St Cewydd's Church, Disserth near Llandrindod Wells; still a very peaceful spot.

Merthyr

One day whilst walking near Carmarthen I was kindly invited to have coffee with a lady who had been churchwarden at the local church of Merthyr. I have to admit that I hadn't walked past the church as it would have meant a detour from the more direct route I had taken. However, she insisted that we visit the church and I was kindly given some information on the history of the site.

The name 'Merthyr' is, of course, usually associated with the big town of Merthyr Tydfil (*Merthyr Tudful*) on the southern edge of the Brecon Beacons. However, the Welsh word is derived from the Latin *martyrium*, meaning a shrine associated with a martyr's death or relics.

In the case of the larger town, the martyr in question is Saint Tydfil (*Tudful* in Welsh), a daughter of Brychan, the fifth-century king who gave his name to Brecon. Tydfil is supposed to have been beheaded by marauding Saxons or Picts, depending on which source you follow. Whoever her killers were, they were presumably pagans making a skirmish into Wales. Just to confuse things further, the name Tydfil suggests a man rather than a woman.

The Merthyr I visited, though, was a tiny place: just the church and a farm and a few houses nearby. The church is dedicated to St Enfael (and also St Martin) but it is unclear whether Enfael is a corruption of Tydfil, and so the village shares the same 'martyr' as its bigger namesake. It could be that Enfael was another martyr from the same kingly family, or, indeed, was the male St Envel, who is associated with Brittany and does not seem to have endured death for his faith.

What does seem clear is that in Welsh this place name does not necessarily mean the burial place of someone who died a violent death in defence of their faith, but may indicate the grave of a saint.

CHAPTER 9

'We're going on an outing'
MORE RECENT CHURCH HISTORY

As I mentioned in Chapter 2, one unexpected event on my pilgrimage was to be taken on an outing. I had got chatting with a couple near Port Talbot who were surprised that I had been in the area but hadn't visited Neath Abbey; a place which is nearby in a car but not if you're on foot. The wife promptly got her car keys and said they would take me to the remains of the Abbey, rather sadly these days on the edge of an industrial estate and close to the M4 motorway. Twenty minutes or so later we arrived at the ruined but still very interesting abbey; in fact part of its charm is the rather unpromising location. It was also lovely to be able to visit this place through the kindness and enthusiasm of strangers.

Neath Abbey was founded in 1130 after the local Norman lord, whose castle was close by in Neath, donated the land to the small Savigniac order from near Coutances in Normandy. However, in 1147 the Savigniacs were absorbed into the larger Cistercian order. Basingwerk Abbey near Holywell, which I also visited, also made this transition, bringing the total number of Cistercian religious houses in Wales to fifteen.

The Cistercians in Wales

We tend to think of Cistercians as occupying remote spots where they could live a life of quiet devotion and provide for themselves through their expertise in agriculture, but this is certainly an oversimplified picture. Neath Abbey was near the coast, in what was a relatively settled area, and Basingwerk was on the Dee estuary, with its ports and wharves. Closer perhaps to what is seen as more typical of the Cistercians are the abbeys of Cwmhir and Cymer, both of which I also visited, the latter being a daughter house of the former.

Cwmhir, which is very ruinous, is still in quite a remote spot in Powys, whereas Cymer is near Dolgellau and on the edge of Snowdonia. I was fortunate in being allowed to camp in the grounds of the abbey at Cwmhir, which even today is just a hamlet surrounded by steep-sided hills. Cymer, on the edge of a broad river valley, seems like a very different place, today being close to quite busy roads.

I saw further, but very different, evidence of Cistercian activity when I was walking on the coastal path south of Aberystwyth. As you walk towards Aberaeron, you can see the remains of monastic fish traps in the sea at low tide. These are quite clearly visible from the height of the coast path, being like small, low enclosures with now very broken-down walls. They were part of an economic network that grew up around medieval religious houses.

But what do we make of these ruined abbeys today? Like all medieval religious houses of Wales and England, their days were ended when Henry VIII brought about the dissolution of the monasteries, a process that started in 1536. This is the main reason why we see them as ruins today. The religious orders that they were part of were banned from operating in England and Wales and the monks (and nuns too in a few cases, two of the Cistercian houses in Wales being communities of women) were pensioned off and in some cases were able to be redeployed in other occupations.

I tend to think that it's helpful to see the religious orders of medieval Europe as the means by which the church of that time renewed itself: the Cistercians themselves were the result of a desire by Benedictine monks to get back to the example of St Benedict, whose Rule, written in about 530, had laid the foundations for monastic life in western Europe.

It is also worth thinking about what the relationship was between the Wales of the early saints and the Cistercians of later medieval Wales. In the information provided by Cadw (the guardians of the site) about the abbey at Cwmhir, the claim is made that the Cistercians are the 'natural successors of the Age of the Saints': a very interesting assertion. They certainly saw themselves as successors to the desert fathers, urged by their own rule to seek out lonely places in which to draw closer to God. In this they echoed the early hermit saints of Wales, who themselves had been influenced by the third- and fourth-century saints of the Egyptian desert. But evidence that they saw themselves as successors to the age of the saints in Wales is limited.

At Margam Abbey, founded in 1147, the Cistercians may have settled on an existing *clas* site, as suggested by several Celtic crosses found there. At Basingwerk, by the thirteenth century the Abbey derived considerable prestige and income from their ownership of the church and well of St Winifred nearby at Holywell. Here the order was clearly happy to reverence the ancient story of St Winifred and encourage pilgrims to visit the miracle-working well. Beyond these examples, however, it would also be interesting to know how much awareness the Cistercians, and perhaps especially their abbots, had of the early Welsh saints and of the Christian heritage of Wales, which was over 600 years old by the time the Cistercians arrived.

But it would also be interesting to know what the impact of the Cistercians on the ordinary people of Wales was. We know they received grants of land and endowments from the wealthy and powerful amongst both Welsh and Anglo-Norman elites, but their impact, and especially their spiritual impact, on the majority of people seems uncertain. They offered prayers and masses for the souls of their wealthy benefactors, but just what was their relationship with ordinary people?

Victorian churches

The Victorians seem to have had rather bad press for over-restoration of medieval churches and also for demolishing what may have been very dilapidated medieval churches and then rebuilding. However, in their defence, I must say that not all Victorian churches in rural Wales are bland lookalikes. One that really impressed me was the village church at Cwmhir Abbey, with its rich tile-work and vivid stained-glass windows. Also, the Victorians were only continuing a tradition of rebuilding. At Cwmhir

Abbey, the previous church had been less than two hundred years old. Usually though, it was medieval churches being replaced; although these too would frequently have been replacements for earlier and simpler buildings, usually made of wood and thatch.

Philanthropy

I visited two churches in the Snowdonia area that had been recipients of considerable wealth from the wife of the local quarry owner, who had made a fortune from the local slate. In one place, the local church had been rebuilt in the nineteenth century with this lady's money; in the second place, her money had provided a new church in what was then a rapidly expanding village[45]. It struck me what amazing generosity and kindness, to say nothing of Christian faith, these churches represented. They were also far from utilitarian buildings, including work in the then fashionable 'arts and crafts' style.

It's easy to be cynical about this kind of giving by the rich, but how much has our country been enriched by the philanthropy of previous generations? This lady could have contented herself with being a wealthy socialite but she didn't do so, perhaps because she knew that such a life would not have brought her contentment. We need to give thanks for those who shared their wealth with not only the less well-off of their own time, but also generations to come.

I also saw evidence of philanthropy in the secular sense when I made an all-too-brief visit to Plas yn Rhiw, a small but beautiful National Trust property on the Llŷn Peninsula between Aberdaron and Abersoch. There, over a cream tea, I learned that the family who had owned it had bought surrounding farmland when it came onto the market. Their intention had been to present the house to the National Trust with as much as possible of the land that had made up the farmstead in earlier times.

CHAPTER 10

'If I wasn't a Christian, I'd have pocketed your £90 and thrown your bag in the sea' CHRISTIAN IDENTITIES

THIS COMMENT WAS recounted rather than said directly to me. The lady concerned had, while on holiday a few years before, gone to a great deal of trouble to locate the owner of a bag she had found containing a considerable amount of money. When she eventually traced and met up with the bag's owner (someone on a bicycle pilgrimage, incidentally), he had asked her if she was a Christian. She had clearly felt quite affronted by this and had made the above comment to him. Perhaps lessons can be learnt from this. Firstly, that many people still identify themselves as Christians; secondly that there is still a strong link in some people's minds between ethical behaviour and Christianity (which is surely a good thing); and, thirdly and perhaps most importantly, that Christians need to be tactful and sensitive when attempting to share their faith. The first two considerations probably apply most to older people. It would be interesting to know how far they still apply to the under-40s, say.

'Are you a Jehovah's Witness?'

One thing that concerns me a lot in my interest in church history is how far the Christian faith extends – not in a geographical sense, but as regards the variety of beliefs amongst those who describe themselves as Christians and the churches and organisations they belong to. Associated with this is the implication that there are some beliefs that are essential, but what exactly are they? And if I, a history graduate who has made a reasonable study of the Christian church through the ages, find these questions difficult, how much more so will Christians whose talents lie in other areas? And what about the 'unchurched' (those who aren't connected to a church), such as the man who asked me if I was a Jehovah's Witness?

When asked this question, I was very surprised but tried to keep this to myself as it was, of course, quite a reasonable request for information. I went on to tell him that I was a Church in Wales Christian, which seemed to satisfy him as an answer and convey to him, I hoped, the sense that I was a member of an 'ordinary' church that he could in some way relate to. However, as the church in its many forms perhaps becomes less mainstream than it seemed a few generations ago, it is quite understandable that many non-churchgoers will find it impossible to differentiate between 'real' Christians and organisations that many would consider to be outside the 'true' church. Thinking about this, I tried to come up with a set of criteria to help someone judge the genuineness of a church or similar organisation. I suspect that none of the 'real' churches would meet all my criteria, but all would meet most of them. The criteria are as follows:

- They use the early church creeds in their services as statements of faith or subscribe to these documents even if they're not used regularly in worship
- They subscribe to the beliefs promoted by the early church councils[46]
- They acknowledge the Bible as a major source of truth and authority and use a version of the Bible also used by other groups
- They are members of the World Council of Churches

- They work with other Christian churches and groups
- They support humanitarian work done by other Christian groups

I would stress that this is my list and I'm open to revising it, but to me it makes sense. Going back to the Jehovah's Witnesses, I think it would be true to say that they meet none of these criteria. I don't say this to dismiss this group; I have known some Witnesses who would put Christians to shame, but I don't see this organisation as being part of historic Christianity.

However, I had a conversation with a Jehovah's Witness on the mid-Wales section of my pilgrimage. We got talking at a campsite, and the lady concerned was interested in what I was doing and freely volunteered that she was a Witness. I wanted to keep the conversation positive, so I mentioned to her that she might like to visit a church nearby with a vast graveyard covering much of a hill – the lady had said she was interested in old graves and their inscriptions. I hinted that the church history that so motivated me could be part of her heritage too, and that she might visit the church as well as the graveyard. For that is what saddens me about many sects and more extreme churches: that their members are cut off from the riches of church history and what it can teach us. The organisation they are members of, by claiming some sort of special revelation, new leader or special text that keeps them apart from Christianity as a whole, deprives people of so much. However, what we need to acknowledge is that people in these organisations are often spiritual seekers just like many of the rest of us. I hope the lady concerned felt that I respected this.

'Are you an Anglican?'

I was asked this by a thoughtful man who was showing me the way to a local campsite. He didn't say anything about his own beliefs or religious allegiances and we soon parted with a warm handshake. I was very aware that the religious and Christian landscape of Wales is very different to that of England. Not only is there the language issue – meaning that some churches are exclusively Welsh speaking, some are just English speaking and many attempt some form of bilingual provision of services – but there has often also been a divide between chapel and church: a divide which still exists today. This was further complicated, or perhaps simplified, by the disestablishment of the Anglican Church in Wales by an Act of Parliament in 1914, meaning that the Queen is not head of the Church in Wales and no Welsh bishops sit in the House of Lords. Disestablishment was the result of the strength of nonconformity in Wales and, in particular, objections to the payment of tithes to the then established church.

I have no idea why my being an Anglican was of particular interest to this man; perhaps I should have asked.

'We try to live our lives by Christian values'

One couple, having told me that they went to church only occasionally, said, 'We try to live our lives by Christian values.' I very much regret not having the courage or presence of mind to ask them what they meant by this. We might consider what 'Christian values' means to us. Something that always worries me about this phrase is that it's often combined with seeing the past in some sort of idyllic light and feeling that Christian faith was stronger in years gone by. This leads on to questions about how we measure faith or the strength of faith in a community or a country. True, if you went back in time fifty or a hundred years, a much larger proportion of the population would have been going to church or chapel regularly and most would have described themselves as Christian. Yet how much of this was just the social norm of the time and driven, at least in part, by the need to seem respectable? How much of the faith of previous generations was real, personal faith and how much was social glue? And what about the surprisingly high number of people in previous generations who did not go to church?

There is also the issue of morality. Various issues tend to be seen as a stage for Christian morality – currently these seem to be the debates surrounding euthanasia and gay marriage. Both these issues are seen by some as being used to erode Christian values. Of course, both these debates are very serious and deserve the consideration of us all. But what about things that were accepted in past generations and yet would horrify us if they took place today?

These could include the slave trade and the widespread use of the death penalty, to say nothing of poverty and very low standards of public health. All of these were assaults on the value of human life and the worth of the individual as a child of God; yet they went on at a time which many of us would look back on and see Britain as a Christian country. Of course, fortunately we have moved on from these things, in part due to the determination of some Christians of those times.

However, we need to see the important issues we face (often arising because of our access to advanced technology) as part of a series of challenging debates that we will have not just now, but into the future. I don't think there is any rose-tinted past we can look back to with nostalgia: the past was just different. And to take another issue rather more recent than the examples given; what about conscription during the First World War? As I walked around Wales, I saw many memorials to the dead of the Great War, made especially poignant by the hundredth anniversary of those terrible events. Many of those who died were conscripts, drafted into the forces from 1916.

It is a great credit to the government of Britain that the possibility of introducing conscription was taken so seriously. People were aware that it would cause real moral dilemmas. Yet in the face of the growing need for men to replace the mass casualties of the war, conscription was introduced for the first time in Britain. But would we tolerate the forced enlistment and great loss of life in Britain today? Would *we* accept such an action on the part of our nation state? I think such a scenario is unthinkable in modern Britain. All in all, a great variety of things can be 'life' issues, and not just the standard ones so beloved of some Christians today.

Going back to that couple, though: perhaps if I had asked them what they meant, they may have said that that they tried to see all people as made in the image of God, that they believed everyone had God-given gifts and abilities, that the vulnerable should be cared for, that those who were criminalised deserved correction and rehabilitation, that lives are meant to be lived in community, and that life is more than acquiring greater comfort for ourselves.

The Orthodox Church in Wales

As there are Orthodox Christians in my own family, I was aware that there was an Orthodox Church in Blaenau Ffestiniog and I was determined to include this in my itinerary. I was warmly welcomed by the priest and able to look around the large church (converted from a former Church in Wales building). I was told that this church has members from a wide area, including many of Russian and eastern-European origins, as well as well as those who have lived locally for generations. Although they're clearly only a small group, there are several Orthodox congregations in Wales, including two Coptic Orthodox churches.

Perhaps because of my family background, I am quite often asked to explain just who the Orthodox are. Many people in western Europe have some vague understanding, based on seeing Greek Orthodox churches on holiday or Russian Orthodox occasionally in the media.

Basically, you have to start with all of 'Christendom' and first put to one side the Roman Catholics, who take the Pope as the head of their church; then also put together and set to one side all the Protestant denominations that date from the Reformation in western Europe (for example the Lutherans of Germany and Scandinavia and the Church of England) and also the churches that then split from them (for example the Presbyterians and the Baptists); then remove all the 'new' churches that have emerged within Protestant Christianity since the Pentecostal and

Charismatic movements of the twentieth century. What you have left then are the Orthodox.

This is a quite a simplified analysis of something that is really much more complex, but it will do for a start. Historically, the Orthodox haven't really featured much in the history of western Europe and many people, including many Christians, are hardly aware of their existence.

It can also be challenging to learn that the church in Wales in the early medieval period is considered to be Orthodox by Orthodox Christians because their final spilt with the Roman Catholic Church did not occur until 1054. Visiting an Orthodox church recently near the English border with Wales, the priest mentioned in his sermon that people are often interested in 'Celtic' saints and spirituality, but often do not grasp that these saints were Orthodox. I think this is a very interesting point and well worth thinking through.

Adoration of the Holy Sacrament

The practice of reserving a communion wafer and keeping or displaying it so that it could be adored as part of worship just wasn't part of my experience. I suppose that I'd come from a background which tended to look on these things as irrelevant or even idolatrous. I think I was also rather wary of the Anglo-Catholic tradition, often feeling more sympathetic to Roman Catholicism. However, in one of the churches I visited there was a leaflet about the Adoration of the Holy Sacrament which explained the usefulness of this practice for worshippers today. It took the tone that we are often rushed, and this includes when we come to Communion at church. As this is a communal celebration, it has to take place within a reasonable amount of time. However, the Adoration of the Sacrament gives us longer – as long as we want really – to dwell on the life of Christ and the significance of His death as an atoning sacrifice, bringing us close to God.

Denominational Labels

Just about anywhere, you can see lots of different places of Christian worship. Some of these may seem unfamiliar, whereas others we can relate to, appreciate or identify with. We may lament the disunity of the universal church, but I believe that Christians can benefit from a greater appreciation of the riches that different church traditions (in the broadest sense) provide. I am blessed to be a member of the Church in Wales with its wealth of history, worship and mission that I can share in, but whatever church background you come from, you have something to share too. If you don't know what it is, do some research on the origins and history of the denomination to which you belong. I am convinced that if we know more of the history, strengths and weaknesses of our own group, our confidence and willingness to work with others will increase and not be diminished.

We may rightly be wary of attempts at to bring about greater church unity by 'top down' negotiation, but let's challenge ourselves to work more with other Christians in our communities and, as individuals and as churches, to work for better understanding and greater appreciation. Also, please don't excuse yourself from this if you belong to a 'new' church – that is, one that has broken away from a more traditional group. It would seem to me that denominational labels can easily persist in these groups. There can also be a tendency to look down on the more traditional or the longer-established churches.

I also think we need to remember that the denominational labels we can sometimes cling on to are increasingly meaningless to the 'unchurched': that is, those with whom we seek to share the hope and joy of the Gospel.

CHAPTER 11

'Have you heard of SongBird Survival?'
THE NATURAL WORLD
AND OUR PLACE IN IT

BEING OFFERED A lift by Derek, who described himself as a farmer and an environmentalist, led to my first conversation that was clearly about ecological issues. He was very involved in a wildlife charity, SongBird Survival[47], and seemed to be especially interested in whether government policies designed to help the environment actually did so. He himself told me that farming and environmentalism, two occupations that are not usually closely associated in the minds of many people, was a perfectly compatible combination.

I would have to admit that in this conversation I got into areas about which I know very little. However, Derek gave various local examples to back up his opinions, which to my untrained mind sounded fairly convincing. Sometime later on my pilgrimage I had another rather similar conversation with an elderly farmer in Snowdonia who also maintained that government schemes intended to benefit the environment often had the opposite effect. In his case one of the examples given was to do with cutting back the reeds in the local river, which he insisted would be detrimental to providing a good habitat for fish.

I like to think that I impressed Derek a little, though. I was able to tell him how amazing the dawn chorus had been after the first night of my pilgrimage at Llanthony. I could only describe it as a wall of sound and, in my ignorance, would certainly have been unable to identify any particular species apart from the call of an owl, which had surprised me at that time of day. I certainly could have done with an expert from SongBird Survival.

On two later occasions on my pilgrimage I again made a note of how lovely the dawn chorus had been as I was waking up. The first of these days was 14 June, in inland Pembrokeshire. I had imagined that by the middle of that month the dawn chorus would be lessening as the birds moved on in their reproductive cycle to rearing their chicks, but this didn't seem to be the case. I wondered whether the birds might be enjoying the uncut grassland and lots of old hedgerows around the site, providing them with plenty of insects on which to feed. Ten days later I again noted the dawn chorus, this time even loud enough to stand up to the noise from the not-so-distant M4 motorway.

In the first week or so on the road, I attempted to make rather amateurish wildlife notes in my diary. This included large numbers of bats at Llanthony, flying around the ruins of the abbey in spite of the chill of early April. The first few days were also marked by the intense humming of vast numbers of bees feeding from the catkins of a particular type of tree. Having now done some research, I think the trees were alders; the black alder being our native species. It had taken me some time to work out where this humming was coming from, which at times was so loud it could have been a distant aircraft. Only as I came down from the Black Mountains on my second day and walked close by one of these trees did I realise what the true reason for this wonderful sound was. The great activity of the bees was, I presume, encouraged by the very warm weather in the daytime, a contrast to close to freezing nights.

I also had a somewhat bee-orientated conversation later in my walk when, in a café in Machynlleth, I got into a conversation with a local beekeeper about ethical issues in apiculture. I was very glad that some time earlier I'd read a magazine article in a consumer journal about the ethics of beekeeping. Later that day, in a stunning little valley in mid Wales, I came across a centre dedicated to researching and breeding queen bees[48]. I did not know such places existed, even though I have a beekeeper for a brother-in-law. That certainly was a very bee-orientated day.

I also managed to see puffins for the first time on my pilgrimage around Wales, from the boat as I went to the island of Bardsey. I saw the birds in flight just a few metres above the water. Seeing these birds was really special for me, as my previous visits to areas of Wales where they are found had always been at the wrong time of year. Being on Bardsey in mid May meant that they were still nesting and rearing their young on cliffs nearby. As soon as this is done, they return to the open sea, where they spend most of the year.

I saw another notable bird species when I visited the Dyfi Osprey Project, run by the Montgomeryshire Wildlife Trust. This project has succeeded in encouraging ospreys, which were for a long time absent from Wales owing to persecution in the nineteenth century, to return and breed. Ospreys are now established in the Dyfi estuary, leaving each year to winter in west Africa and then returning to rear their young in Wales. I got there too late in the day to do anything except watch the birds on CCTV in the small visitor centre, but this suited me fine and I got a great view. In this area of Wales, it was also very encouraging to repeatedly hear the call of the cuckoo.

An unexpected wildlife encounter very different to the majestic osprey or the colourful puffin was finding a small, rather elegant moth in the Ladies one evening at a campsite on the Pembrokeshire coast. Looking this up later at home, it turned out to be a White Ermine moth, which I was informed is quite common in Britain, although I had certainly never seen this lovely creature before.

I also was struck at times by the more long-term forces of nature. One fascinating leaflet I picked up near the coast in north-east Wales was entitled 'Pebbles along the beach'. This small but very informative bit of tourist literature, produced by Denbighshire and Flintshire County Councils, was different to anything I've ever seen. It briefly described the origins of igneous, sedimentary and metamorphic rocks, something I was reasonably aware of from 'O' level geography at school. However, this was followed by clear, labelled photos of pebbles on local beaches, describing which category of rock they belonged to and how they had found their way, since the last ice age, to the coast of north Wales.

My appreciation of geology was also extended a month or so later when I walked on the beach at Newgale (*Niwgwl*) in Pembrokeshire. Having pitched my tent, I could see that the tide was far out, enabling me to walk north-westwards on the beach and get a good view of the wonderful rock formations of the cliffs.

Ten days or so later I again saw cliffs in a new light. I had often noticed the steep escarpment to the landward side of the M4 motorway near Port Talbot, but it was only when walking through nearby Aberavon (*Aberafan*) that I found out from a local information board on the seafront that the steep hillside just beyond the motorway had in fact been sea cliffs at the end of the last ice age. The current shoreline about two miles away is the result of a build-up of sand and pebbles in the last 10,000 years or so. I was also especially fascinated to learn that the huge build-up of sand dunes at nearby Kenfig (*Cynffig*) and the complete loss of the medieval village and church there, could be at least in part explained by exceptional tides in the fifteenth century. Information at the site said that tides in 1433 were of a height that would only occur once every 1,700 years.

As I walked I was grateful for information boards and other sources that improved my very slight knowledge of the natural world. I was frequently confronted by my own ignorance, but I like to think that as I made progress on my pilgrimage, I also gained a greater appreciation of nature.

The view of southern Snowdonia from Criccieth Castle in north Wales.

Green Christian?

Shortly before I set out on my trek, I'd been in conversation with one of my sisters, who is involved in editing the magazine, *Green Christian*[49]. She suggested to me that I could perhaps write an article for the magazine after I completed my pilgrimage. Flattered though I was to be asked, I never imagined that I would have sufficient to write about on relevant themes. In fact it was only much later, as I passed the vast steelworks at Port Talbot, that such an article began to form in my mind.

Perhaps one obvious 'green' theme on my walk is that I travelled on foot, using local services – mainly campsites and village shops – as I went. So it was definitely slow travel and I like to think that my carbon footprint wasn't too big, although my husband turning up in the camper van certainly increased it. I have since speculated about whether in the future I could make a similar trip without a support vehicle. I think that I could do so, but I would need to organise myself rather differently, mainly as regards getting some laundry done and getting internet access.

Being away for three months and my slow walking pace also enabled me to observe the changing seasons, different landscapes and very different habitats in a way that most of us do not get to in our ordinary lives. A very sunny April with cold nights gave me the opportunity to

141

wake up in temperatures which were sometimes below freezing. Chilly May days saw me wearing my winter clothes until nearly the end of the month. I saw the bluebells come and go, the wild garlic arrive and the cow parsley grow tall.

Walking past the huge steelworks at Port Talbot was perhaps a turning point for me in my consideration of green issues. I had passed the steelworks on many occasions driving down the M4 motorway and they had long had a fascination for me, their starkness being strangely appealing. I had looked forward to walking past them.

On my pilgrimage I certainly did not want to shut out the obviously man-made, the ugly and the polluting. Even on the second day of my pilgrimage, walking in the glorious Black Mountains near my home, I was struck by the contrast between the lovely, unspoilt hills and the other valleys of the industrial areas of south Wales. These other valleys were not far away, just up the Heads of the Valleys road. Until about 250 years ago, the industrial valleys of south Wales would have been very much like the mountain landscape which so delighted me that day.

Of course it was lovely to see the natural world in all its glory; the magnificent escarpment of the Black Mountains above Glasbury, the large number of seals on the north Wales coast and the boulder-strewn Wye above Builth Wells. But passing steelworks, reservoirs and forests, it would be wrong not to reflect on my own use of steel, my own requirement for a steady supply of water from a drowned valley and my own use of products from vast conifer plantations.

I also saw a little of the challenge of transforming what had been an industrial landscape into something that can be restored and enjoyed now and in the future. A few weeks before Port Talbot, I'd crossed the river Ystwyth, which used to be very polluted due to old lead and zinc mines upstream. However, an information board described the considerable progress that has been made in reducing pollutants in what is now lovely country for walking, cycling and fishing. I had also walked through the stunning coastal park that runs for miles in what were industrial areas around Llanelli. We can rejoice in the power of nature and the possibilities for renewal.

But what I consider most 'green' about my pilgrimage is that I took time out, a sabbatical even. In a world where being busy is almost a status symbol, it was a privilege to be able to take three months away from ordinary life.

Lake Vyrnwy

I saw several very interesting but relatively modern stained-glass windows in various churches on my pilgrimage. One that I found particularly poignant was the window in memory of George Frederick Deacon, who designed the dam at Lake Vyrnwy. His memorial, in the church of St Wddyn in Llanwddyn, depicts the Old Testament story where Moses is told 'You shall strike the rock, and water will come out of it, that the people may drink' (Exodus 17:6, in the *New American Standard Bible*), although the text that is included in the window, 'I will give you living water', is an adaptation of the story of the Samaritan woman at the well from John's Gospel.

These Biblical stories perhaps help to highlight some of the issues and circumstances surrounding the building of the dam, which was the first stone dam of its type, creating the biggest artificial lake in Europe at that time. The valley of the River Vyrnwy (*Afon Efyrnwy*), a tributary of the River Severn, was chosen because the bedrock was sufficiently strong to provide a foundation for the dam. The cities (in this case Liverpool) of an increasingly industrial and urban Britain needed a clean and reliable source of water, and Lake Vyrnwy became the first of many reservoirs created in Wales to serve cities and towns not just in England but in Wales too. These drowned valleys have had a massive impact on the landscape of Wales.

The church of St Wddyn is itself part of the relatively new village of Llanwddyn, built by the Corporation of Liverpool to house the displaced villagers, the dam being completed in 1888 and the church consecrated the same year. The church was one of the first in Britain to have electric light, as one of the requirements placed on the Liverpool Corporation was that the building should be supplied with hydro-electricity as a by-product of the dam.

Another issue that was raised in conversation when I visited the dam was the care of the human remains buried in the old graveyard, now under the waters of the lake. One lady I spoke to was very concerned about what may have happened to the bodies in the old graves. However, this was all taken care of in the planning of the new dam, and all remains down to a depth of seven feet were removed and reinterred with their gravestones at the new church.

Lake Vyrnwy in mid Wales with its picturesque Victorian straining tower, where the water is drawn off to go by pipeline to Liverpool, 70 miles away.

CHAPTER 12

'What do you think about when you're walking?' A SPIRITUAL JOURNEY

THIS WAS PERHAPS the most challenging question I was asked on my whole walk, the enquirer being a hospitable campsite owner who had invited me to have breakfast with her. Nobody else ever asked me a question like it; perhaps our thoughts are considered to be private. The question certainly took me aback, but I attempted to answer as truthfully as possible. I was at that time only a few days into my pilgrimage and not used to sharing what I was doing, but I decided I had to be upfront with her and say that I prayed some of the time as I walked; I added that I try to pray for a specific group of people each day. This lady kindly took my honesty in her stride and told me that she prayed too, which was obviously encouraging. She then wanted to know if I sometimes walked without thinking, 'just striding along'. This certainly was the case, but I told her I also had plenty of 'I must just get to the top of this hill'-type thoughts. I also had map-reading and looking at the landscape-type thoughts. But what I knew I really must say was that I had depressive-type thoughts too. When I added this into the conversation, it was a risk; but I needn't have worried as this kind person seemed quite able to cope with my admissions of weakness. Fortunately she was too tactful to ask for details.

I noticed throughout my walk that negative feelings often set in when I was tired, or anxious about finding a campsite.

The negativity was usually in the form of anger at people I felt had misjudged me or overlooked me. Unfortunately I had had a string of incidents in the then quite recent past where I felt I had been treated this way, and these episodes fuelled my depressive feelings. Although these things were now behind me, I still struggled with the pain that I had felt. I knew it wasn't a good place to be in as I walked on my pilgrimage, and neither was it a good basis for life in our new church family, but I still felt very vulnerable at times. Ironically perhaps, as my walk progressed and I neared the end, my depressive thoughts deepened. I had felt a growing confidence in my own abilities and I felt a certain pride in what I had achieved – hopefully the right sort of pride. However, in my depressive moments this further fuelled my resentment that *they* could so belittle and undermine me, someone who had walked around Wales. It was then that I knew I needed to deal with the problem for my own sake, let alone the sake of anybody else.

I gradually came to a more peaceful frame of mind through various means. One was to appreciate that when I was dwelling on these thoughts, I couldn't pray. It was simply impossible to do so, as the negativity took over mind entirely. I began to see that although I saw myself as on a prayer walk and, indeed, felt a growing call to intercessory prayer, I couldn't do the very thing that I wanted to do. I also began to see a pattern of negativity in my relationships with others, which had grown up because of various factors. I realised I needed to be free from this pattern and allow God to build up my confidence and the right sort of assertiveness. On good days I could see that what God was leading me into was far more exciting than any negativity I had been trapped in. I also began to pray for those who had hurt me in the past. This became one of the weapons in my armoury as I countered the negativity in my mind. All of this was only ever a series of battles. I never got to the stage where I felt I had won the war.

'Do you have a job, or do you see *this* as a vocation?'

These were perhaps amongst the most encouraging words spoken to me on my pilgrimage. They were spoken by a lady over coffee after a church service near Aberystwyth. She was a retired head teacher and recently widowed, and clearly someone who had a considerable, although quiet, ministry in her church. I think her words meant so much because I *was* feeling a growing sense of vocation, and I was encouraged that she seemed to sense this.

I was fortunate perhaps that I had been old enough (I celebrated my 57th birthday during my pilgrimage) to have taken early retirement from teaching. This gave me some justification for taking three months out of ordinary life and going on something of an adventure now that I was newly released from actively earning a living. However, I had had a growing sense of vocation over the previous year or so. Prayer had always been important to me, but I found I was increasingly called to intercessory prayer.

In the church we'd belonged to before moving to Wales, I had begun to do more ministry-type tasks. However, as we planned our move and went up to Wales house-hunting, we'd also seen that the local churches were reorganising and needing to move into more shared ministry with a greater role for lay people. This was a further encouragement to me. Soon after we moved, I was able to renew my licence as a 'Lay Minister' in the local diocese and get more actively involved in ministry.

My pilgrimage had also grown out of my desire to go on a longer prayer walk. I'd increasingly been drawn into prayer walking and taking mini-retreats in local places, organising a programme for myself and thinking through and praying for various situations. I felt a very clear sense of vocation to go on a longer prayer walk and this sense grew during my journey.

I was first able to share something of my vocation with one of the St Asaph pilgrims, who was a retired clergyman and leader of retreats. He was a great encouragement to me and took my feelings seriously: my wondering about what my vocation was, and even whether I was being led to become a hermit. Spending time in Aberdaron at the end of the walk across north Wales gave me another unexpected chance to consider this calling when I found out that the local church included a hermit as part of the church family. This gave me just a tiny opportunity to consider the practicalities of such a vocation. Whether I am led in this way remains to be seen, but I don't think I have any doubt that God is leading me in prayer walking as a vocation at the current time.

I had felt this very much around the time we moved to Wales, just a few months before I set out on my pilgrimage. I started a series of prayer walks in my local area, praying for the local churches and about other issues. I divided the ten churches in our local area into four groups and set off on a series of walks over a few months. This was a really good way to get to know the local area better and helped me engage with places in a spiritual way.

I was therefore really encouraged by the remark made by this lady, which I saw as confirmation of what God was doing in my life. It wasn't that I hadn't felt a sense of vocation in my old job as a teacher; in fact I saw this time and the wonderful opportunities it gave me very much as a calling from God. Seeing my old job in that way helped me to move onto something new as God called me to it. Above all, I think we all need to feel God's call and purpose in our lives.

'That will be a bit of a culture shock'

At this point I was discussing with someone my need to get home by early July as I had relatives arriving to stay from New Zealand and needed to get organised for their visit. The person I was in conversation with quite rightly thought that this would be quite a culture shock after three months on the road and only the most rudimentary domestic life. But I think he was also thinking beyond this, to the fact that being at home again and coping with ordinary life would be quite a challenge.

His comment made me think about the advantages there would be to going home. Firstly, I knew it would be lovely to be with my husband each day. I'd also be able to do things that were impractical to do on a pilgrimage, such as baking and using the computer. I'd be able to eat a wider variety of food. I'd also be able to catch up with my family after only very sporadic contact for a few months. I'd be able to be hospitable and have people round for meals.

There would be other simple things like being able to wear different types of clothes to my quite utilitarian pilgrim outfit. I would also know that there was no real reason why I couldn't do something similar again, and I'd shown myself how much I benefitted from some time out. Additionally, I'd have my home church's services and other events to go to and chance to get to know our new 'church family' better. Yes, of course, it would be a culture shock, but not one without many compensations.

The Gay Christian issue

My own spiritual journey as I walked also took me to places in my mind and faith that I hadn't considered very much before.

One issue which I came across several times on my pilgrimage was that of homosexuality in relation to Christian faith. I have to admit that this is not something which I have had direct contact with; however, the months when I was walking coincided with various meetings organised by dioceses across Wales to discuss the issue of whether same-sex marriage should be allowed in the Church in Wales. I came across relevant literature in several churches, outlining the different views on this issue. I was also interested to find out at one church that I visited that a previous vicar had been the founder of the Gay and Lesbian Christian movement[50]. I have to admit that I was quite out of my comfort zone with this. However, as a divorced and remarried person who did not have a church wedding for their second marriage, I think I am prepared to consider the case of same-sex couples who wish to marry in church. I still feel some sense of annoyance at the vicar who said that my second marriage 'probably wouldn't be allowed'.

Now, twenty years on, divorced people marrying in church has become more acceptable; perhaps same-sex marriage will go the same way.

Seeing the patterns in our lives

One small church I visited had a notice of welcome to visitors asking them to 'Trace the patterns in the decoration of this building. Realise that God is there in the pattern of your own life.'

I, all too often, see painful patterns in my own life. They are patterns, going back to childhood, of feeling ignored, of being on the end of disparaging remarks and not knowing what, if anything, to say. This pattern then leads to a showdown where I confront those who have put me down. Sometimes this showdown has been real; sometimes it just exists in my own imagination, where it is carefully reworked. How I have envied those who can so freely enjoy life, who seem untouchable to the 'put downers'.

But however painful the patterns of life may seem, this doesn't have to be the only pattern that I see. I can also see a pattern where God has protected me from things far worse than what I actually experienced or even imagined. I can see a pattern where God was drawing me to Himself long before I was aware of Him. I can see a pattern where people who knew Him came across my path, such as the cleaning lady who worked for my mother giving me a second-hand New Testament on my tenth birthday. I have long since lost or given away that little Bible, but how I wish I could get it back. Also the nun who offered to pray with me when I was stranded alone in Paris aged 14. I refused her offer, having no understanding of prayer or a caring God.

I can see now that both the difficult things and the good things were being woven together to make the pattern of my life as it is today. And it is a pattern that God is still working on.

Don't speed on the beach at Porthmadog!

Bibliography

These are the main sources I drew upon in writing this book.

Burton, J and Stöber, K: *Abbeys and Priories of Medieval Wales* (University of Wales Press, 2015)

Davies, W: *Wales in the Early Middle Ages* (Leicester University Press, 1982)

Davies, W L: *Welsh Metrical Versions of the Psalms* (*Journal of the Welsh Bibliographical Society* Vol. 2, no. 8, 1923)

Davis, P: *Sacred Springs: in Search of the Holy Wells and Spas of Wales* (Blorenge Books, 2003)

Dyfed Archaeological Trust: *Medieval and Early Post-Medieval Holy Wells: Additional sites* (Cadw, 2012)

Evans, E: *Early Medieval Ecclesiastical Sites in South-East Wales* (Cadw, 2003)

Hare Preservation Trust, The (Russ, J ed),: *The Hare Book* (Graffeg, 2015)

Hughes, T J: *Wales's Best One Hundred Churches* (Seren, 2007)

Jones, F: *The Holy Wells of Wales*, 3rd edn. (University of Wales Press, 1992)

Morton, A: *Trees of the Celtic Saints* (Gwasg Carreg Gwalch, 2009)

Price, H: *A new edition of the Historia Divae Monacellae* (Welsh Journals Online. Montgomeryshire Collections Vol. 82, 1994)

Procter, E: *Llanthony Priory in the Vale of Ewyas: The Landscape Impact of a Medieval Priory in the Welsh Marches* (dissertation for MSc in Applied Landscape Archaeology), 2007

Seaborne, M: *Celtic Crosses of Britain and Ireland*, 2nd edn. (Shire Publications Ltd, 1989)

Touchstone Heritage Management Consultants & Associates: *Celtic Saints, Spiritual Places and Pilgrimage* (Cadw, 2011)

Welch, S: *Making a Pilgrimage* (Lion Hudson, 2009)

Endnotes

1   This term, often used for the area along the Welsh/English border, is believed to be derived from the Norman French word for a frontier area. It is often used of the English counties of Herefordshire and Shropshire, and sometimes also the adjoining areas of Wales.

2   This is from *The Canterbury Tales* and is found in the Prologue (line 9). However, in Chaucer's time, Pentecost rather than Easter was traditionally seen as the start of the pilgrimage season, and this festival usually falls in May. Chaucer's comments perhaps reflect people's eager anticipation of pilgrimage. What it is important to understand, though, are the very limited opportunities for travel in medieval times. Pilgrimage was the main reason for travel by ordinary people, who were generally required to stay in their home parish.

3   This is the name often given to the period of three centuries or so starting roughly from the end of the fourth century, when the Romans left Wales. This was a time when many churches and religious communities were founded in Wales and the ordinary people were Christianised.

4   This was the North Wales Pilgrim's Way. See http://www.pilgrims-way-north-wales.org/ I am very grateful to the North Wales Pilgrims, associated with St Asaph's Cathedral, for all their help to me.

5   This classification is for roads less than four metres in width. The broken lines indicate an unfenced road.

6   There are currently sixteen National Trails in England and Wales. The most famous is probably the Pennine Way, which was inaugurated in 1965.

7   Green lanes are often in the 'other routes with public access' category on OS maps. See the Ordnance Survey website or OS maps for details. These are generally old roads that are just 'hanging on' as part of the road network.

8   'Religious house' is a general term for an institution of monks, nuns or priests living under some sort of community rule.

9   This story comes from the time of Norman consolidation of power in this area of Wales. Having famously won the Battle of Hastings in 1066, the Normans soon moved into south-east Wales, obviously easily accessible from England. Abergavenny Castle a few miles away, built by the Norman lord Hamelin de Ballon around 1087, was built to defend Norman rule in this area.

10   The Augustinians followed precepts drawn up by St Augustine in the late fourth century. These encouraged a life based on the ideals of poverty, chastity and obedience.

11   The Latin word *hospitium* has 'morphed' into *ysbyty* in Welsh and into 'hospice'/'hospital' in English. In Latin it means the place where guests are received and cared for, and the caring hospitality itself.

12   This was the Upper Cwmbran to Henllys section of the Torfaen Trail, promoted by Torfaen Borough Council. See www.torfaen.gov.uk

13   I would describe my sleeping bag as being suitable for 'Wales at Easter'. I already owned a bag I would call suitable for 'Scotland at Easter', but this was too bulky and heavy to take on a longer walk and would probably have been too warm much of the time.

14   This is The Gideons International, an international Christian organisation which distributes Bibles and New Testaments in schools, hospitals and so on. See www.gideons.org.uk

15   *The Radicalisation of Bradley Manning*, by the Welsh playwright Tim Price, was first performed in 2012. Bradley Manning, a US soldier, had then recently been convicted of crimes against the Espionage Act in that he had released large quantities of sensitive material related to the wars in Iraq and Afghanistan. Manning, whose mother was Welsh, had lived in Wales as a teenager and attended secondary school in Haverfordwest. The play draws on how his experiences in Wales contributed to his social isolation and radicalisation. Bradley Manning is now a transgender woman with the name Chelsea Manning.

16   In the words of the BBC, this is a new paper 'aimed at people who are short of time'. BBC News 26/10/10

17   There is considerably more detail on the '25,000' maps, which makes them ideal for walkers. In the words of Ordnance Survey, '1:25,000 scale means 4 cm on a map equal 1 km on the ground'. www.ordnancesurvey.co.uk
     I find it interesting to reflect that OS maps (a national treasure in

my opinion) originated in the Napoleonic Wars in response to the military need for accurate mapping.

18   Perhaps relevant to this is the observation that it is in the four corners of Wales that you find lower-lying, more usable land, the central areas being mountainous and very rugged with more than a quarter of the land over 1000 feet in altitude.

19   The early medieval period in Welsh history goes from the end of Roman rule to the coming of the Normans following William the Conqueror's accession to the throne of England in 1066.

20   This twelfth-century *Life* now survives only in later revisions. See *A new edition of the Historia Divae Monacellae* by Huw Price, Welsh Journals Online. Montgomeryshire Collections, Vol. 82, 1994.

21   The rood screen was a partition which screened the chancel (i.e. the priests' section of the church) from the nave (i.e. the people's section) in many medieval churches. Rood screens are discussed more fully in the chapter 'On being a church visitor'.

22   This was the Rug chapel near Corwen in north Wales. With the same ticket you can also visit Llangar Old Parish Church, which is about a mile away – or better still join Cadw to get free access to all historic sites in Wales in their care. See www.cadw.gov.wales

23   *The Tablet*, July 5th 1913

24   *Clas* churches are dealt with in more detail in Chapter 8.

25   See the websites of Bardsey Lodge and Bird Observatory and the Bardsey Island Trust at www.bardsey.org and www.bbfo.org.uk respectively.

26   The very remarkable collection of ancient crosses and stones at Llantwit Major includes the beautiful Houelt's Cross, which is a disc-headed cross with a Latin inscription and Celtic-style decoration and is believed to date from the ninth century. Information at the site describes how these early Celtic inscribed stones 'speak of saints and kings educated at Llanilltud Fawr'.

27   Vivien Kelly reporting an unknown source, in the preface to lectures published following a conference at Llantwit Major in 2000.

28   This was a newsletter entitled *Church Matters* produced by Ecclesiastical Insurance, and made very interesting reading. It was dated September 2013.

29   This church is surrounded by land owned by the National Trust, who also provide a car park nearby.

30   This is actually an oversimplification. In some medieval churches in England the rood screen was about a third of the way down what we would consider to be the nave, such as at the parish church in Dunster in Somerset. I am not aware of any parish churches in Wales which had the same arrangement.

31   This may have been influenced by the revolt in Devon and Cornwall in 1549 which was, in part, the result of the imposition of the English prayer book in areas where Cornish was spoken.

32   The National Eisteddfod is the annual Welsh cultural festival. The first official National Eisteddfod of modern times was held in Aberdare in south Wales in 1861. Although it has nearly always been held in Wales, in the early twentieth century several were held in the Liverpool and Birkenhead area, which is close to north Wales and home to considerable Welsh communities.

33   This was Waterfront Korean Church.

34   The book was *Trees of the Celtic Saints – The Ancient Yews of Wales*, by Andrew Morton. In spite of my concerns about extra weight, it is a slim but fascinating volume.

35   Bede in his *Ecclesiastical History of England* quotes a letter from Pope Gregory in which Gregory advises that missionary efforts in England are more likely to succeed when people 'may the more freely resort to the places to which they have been accustomed'. Bede's eighth-century history is available online at www.ccel.org.

36   When I made another visit later, most of the small items had been taken away.

37   There were many examples of this practice in the ancient world and it also continues into our own times, such as people throwing coins into wishing wells and fountains.

38   Francis Jones in *The Holy Wells of Wales* (p. 32) lists six wells attributed to St Beuno, all in north Wales.

39   Francis Jones attributes 32 wells to David/Dewi, all in west or mid Wales. Glamorgan, with three wells associated with the saint, seems to have been on the edge of David's sphere of influence. In contrast, Jones gives 18 as the number of Pembrokeshire wells associated with David.

40   The website of St Hywyn's Church in Aberdaron includes very interesting information about these stones. See www.st-hywyn.org.uk.

41   There is some more up-to-date information about this church on the website www.britishlistedbuildings.co.uk.

42   The *Geiriadur Prifysgol Cymru* (University of Wales dictionary) defines *clas* – plural *clasau* – as 'monastic community, *monastica classis*, convent, body of collegiate clergy or canons common in the church in Wales in pre-Norman times; cloister; college'.

43   The books were *The Settlements of the Celtic Saints in Wales* (1954) and *Saints, Seaways and Settlements in the Celtic Lands* (1969).

44   What is interesting about Benedictine religious houses in Wales is that they were founded soon after the Norman Conquest in the late eleventh and early twelfth centuries, and were often associated with the establishment of power by Norman lords. I also visited the former Benedictine houses at Ewenny and Kidwelly, both parish churches since the Reformation.

45   These were the churches at Maentwrog and Blaenau Ffestiniog.

46   This is the series of Church councils attended by what we would call today the Roman Catholic and Orthodox churches, held between the fourth and eighth centuries. The most famous statement resulting from these councils is the Nicene Creed of 325.

47   SongBird Survival supports research into the reasons for the decline of songbirds and other small birds in Britain. See www.songbird-survival.org.uk.

48   This was the West Wales Bee Breeding Project at Maesycoed, north of Aberystwyth.

49   *Green Christian* magazine is the journal of Christian Ecology Link. See www.greenchristian.org.uk.

50   This was Jim Cotter, who was the organisation's first General Secretary.

Also from Y Lolfa:

JAMES PIERCE

The Life
and Work of
William
Salesbury

A RARE SCHOLAR

yLolfa

£14.99

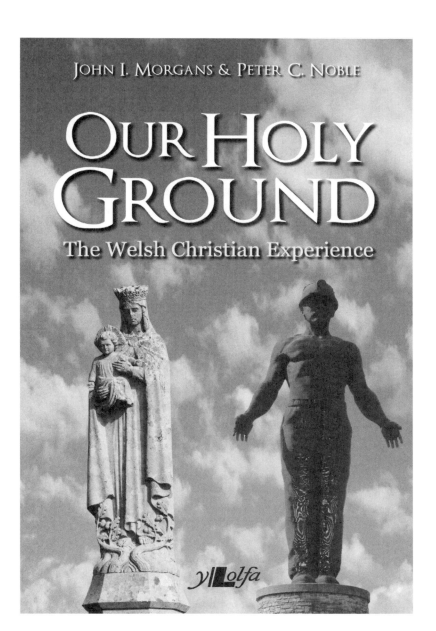

JOHN I. MORGANS & PETER C. NOBLE

OUR HOLY GROUND

The Welsh Christian Experience

y Lolfa

£9.99